ISBN 978-1-5283-9194-8
PIBN 11004998

Forgotten Books is a registered trademark of FB &c Ltd.
Copyright © 2018 FB &c Ltd.
FB &c Ltd, Dalton House, 60 Windsor Avenue, London, SW19 2RR.
Company number 08720141. Registered in England and Wales.

For support please visit www.forgottenbooks.com

1 MONTH OF
FREE
READING

at
www.ForgottenBooks.com

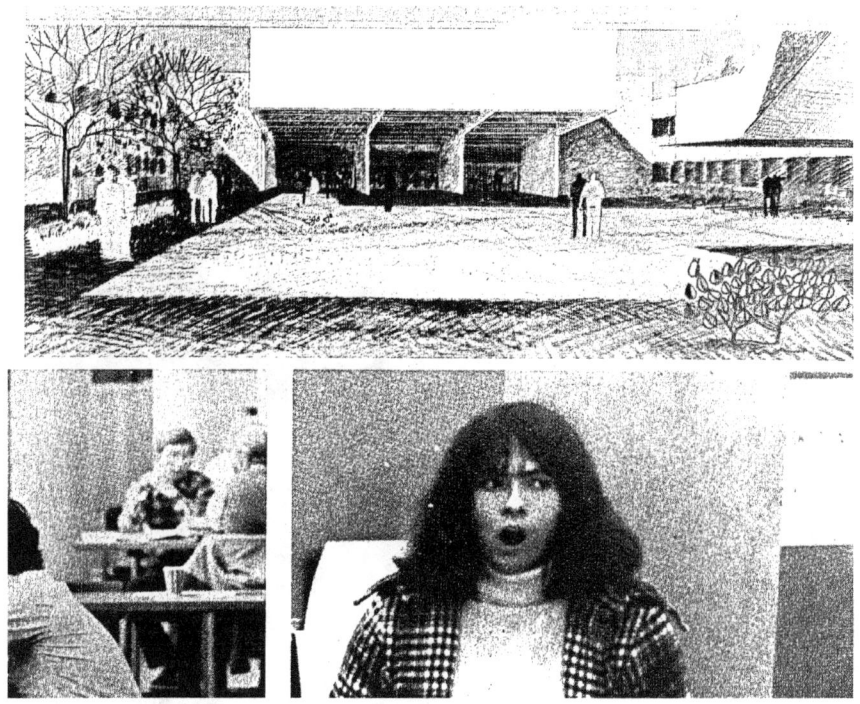

photo essay by dennis trowbridge

"YOU KNOW WHAT?"
Hey, you know what?
I can smell winter coming,
Yeah, even with a head-cold.
This morning when I woke up,
As I was walking to work.
I could really feel it in the air,
Somewhere just hiding behind fall's
Brownish faded trench-coat.
                    —Robin Davis

FALL

Slowly seeping into proud trees
Life's silent loneliness prevails on them
To cry their greenish youth away,
As mellow leaves upon a dying earth.
                    —Robin Davis

windestate
-a short story complete on these two pages
by etha griffin

The trees stood courageously, refusing to yield to the wanton wind, so the wind gave up and breezed away. It was going to be that kind of day.

The grass sighed a sufficiently grass-like sigh, and the few spring flowers available for comment merely straightened up and stretched a stamen here or a pistil there.

The rocks, of course, didn't sigh in fact, it was rare indeed when a rock said or did anything of any consequence. Canton, as he trod through the trees, thought he heard something like grass sighing, and he wondered at the sudden scarcity of that abounding abstraction, the wind.

Moment before, as the rabbit had stood smiling, and the blades of grass had come to rest, Canton had noticed the absense of the ruffling wind. And yet here, in the midst of a seemingly unwindy stretch of forest stood a still-operated windmill, operating without the apparent aid of the wind.

Canton sat down on a dead log chich conveniently faced the whirling windmill. Actually, the log was not dead, and in fact was not even a log but rather the living, sapping, growing trunk of a decrepitly ancient and gnarled oak tree. Of course, this old oak was bent beyond hope of ever straightening up, which explains Canton's chair chosen position atop it, but does not explain why it's bent.

Canton leaned back against the curving trunk and closed his eyes. Shadows fell on his face accompanied by an occasional inch-worm, as he slept. And Canton slept even as the minute scrap of paper bit his cheek and fell limpidly to the ground beside him. Next a brass letter-opener found its animated way to his side, and it was followed by an aluminum hinge off a garage door which was followed closely by a half-full bottle of coke.

The clang caused by the aluminum hinge striking the brass letter opener awakened Canton, and immediately his curiosity was aroused. Aroused neither by the calendar with its underterminable dates not by the mere fact that an unrelated pile of refuse and found its way to his side, but by the half-full bottle of coke. The immediate question is his still slumbering mind had to do with the temperature of the caramel liquid. Canton merely wondered if the coke was cold enough to drink without ice. It was, so he drank it.

Then, upon finding relief for his parched throat, he sought relief for his parched mind. No easy task. The calendar proved to be no source of entertainment, Canton realized, because he already knew the date, but the crumpled note caught his eye and he grasped for it, only to have it move off, under the influence of the windmill, out of his reach. Undaunted, he sprung from his trunk-seat and landed with his right foot squarely planted on the unsuspecting message.

Canton reached down and removed the paper from beneath his shoe. shook some of the dried mud from it, and opened it up to read. It said: "And so I write this to you, Lord Dunsary, unsuspecting as you are of the assasination plans, hoping that it will reach you before the assasins do. God speed, My Lord, and . . ." That was all, the note ended as abruptly as it had started.

Canton sat down and tried to piece some semblence of intelligence to the note, but it escaped all snatches of sanity, and its meaning seemed to

That sweet spring smell, nati to energy part of the country during the pre-summer season, flooded Canton's nose. And Canton smiled. A rabbit leaning against one of the few remaining elm tree smiled back at Canton, wrinkling its nose in a characteristically herbivorous smile. Canton, not noticing the grinning rabbit, kept on walking and breathing. And as he was walking and breathing his eyes rose from the forested carpet to the clearing directly before him. (Isn't there always a clearing?) The clearing contained a small, operating windmill located in a clearing. But he should have, because just a wither further still under Canton's curious gaze. Canton didn't know of any Lord Dunsary, but the implied murder frightened him. And it was then that he noticed for the first time, the odd movement of the circling windmill. Odd, Canton realized, because of the lack of a wind-like factor to justify and sustain its movement.

The windmill swung its wooden arms contemptuously, and Canton's stared after them in sudden disbelief. He turned to retrieve the letter opener, and considering the absurdity of the moment, did an utterly absurd thing. He reached out for the letter opener grasping it as one might a sword, and marched determined towards the relentlessly rotating windmill.

Upon reaching its door he knocked twice, while dodging massive windmill blows, but he received no answer. And since he received none, he pushed his way inside. His eyes, having a little trouble adjusting to the internal darkness soon altogether regretted their enlightening process

AH! THE SEASONS!

Ah! Winter ends!
The old snow-clouds
All melt away
To the sea-sky!
Ah! Spring begins!
The new green shoots
Break through the skin
Of the brown earth!
Ah! Summer comes!
The cool stream runs
Like a moist vein
Through dry terrain!
Ah! Fall returns!
The low sun beams
As its rays turn
Red the blue seas!

—w. h. watling, jr.
18 february 1973

photo by dennis trowbridge

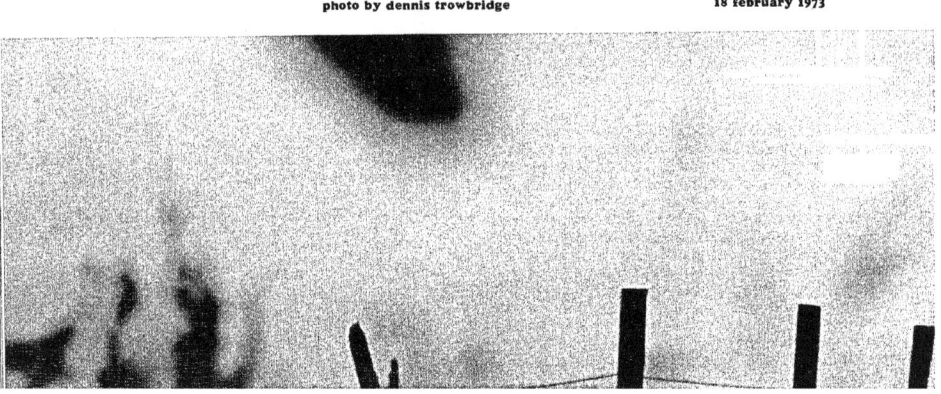

- jane ballou, Oct. 7

and so it went ....

HELP

TO   Joliet Junior College Board, District 525

FROM: Edward Peltzhoover, President, Junior College Council, Local 604

RE   An open request

I should like to request respectfully that the Junior College Board, District 525, re-examine the "Joliet Educational Agreement" with District 204. Although the stated desire in the agreement--"to expand educational services to the greatest number of citizens"--is consistent with existing faculty desires, the following are of grave concern

1 Item four on page two states that District 204 "will function as the administrative arena" for "the employment of teaching personnel." Since the Board approves part-time teaching personnel to execute the instructional program, is it, in this agreement, abrogating its normal responsibilities and possibly violating its own institutional integrity?

2 Item four also states that District 204 will hire supervisory personnel Not having served in the curriculum process on campus, will these supervisory personnel assure the 525 Board that standards of quality will be met? Is there any assurance in the agreement that courses offered will have the slightest resemblance to those offered in the normal program? If not, will student-earned credit be placed in jeopardy? Is the institution fair in its package?

3 Since only a little better than a year ago the Junior College received its North Central accreditation, which resulted from an evaluation of this faculty these facilities, and the administrative structure, will the agreement not raise questions about what it was we were really being evaluated to do? Might the same be asked of certification from the Illinois Junior College Board?

Please understand, we support the principle of expanding educational opportunity We do, however, have serious reservations about the implementation of this Agreement which

  a Appears to relieve the elected officials of this college from its
     normal duties and responsibilities

  b May place student-earned credit in jeopardy

  c May place this institution in the academic vending business

                JOLIET JUNIOR COLLEGE

October 5, 1973

To   All faculty

From   Richard Zwielach
        Chief Negotiator, District 525

We think it is important for you to know that the Board will be making a monetary proposal to Local 604, A. F. T. on Thursday, October 11, 1973. The proposal will include all monetary items including work load and fringe benefits. The union negotiators have been informed that the offer would be forthcoming at that time. we are taking this method of notifying you at the latest A. F. T. memorandum failed to mention this important point.

October 10, 1973

To   All Faculty Members
From   P D bcАninch, President
Re   Student Petition

At the Board meeting Monday night the Board was presented with a petition signed by 69 students indicating that certain teachers are using the classroom to discuss negotiations from the A F T point of view The students expressed the concern that they are in effect a captive audience and hear only the one point of view. They wish to hear both sides of the issue

I recognize that in the heat of the negotiations process, emotions run high and some faculty members can be led into inappropriate classroom discussions of noon eating issues about which they feel very strongly At the same time, however I am sure we would agree that students have a basic right to the course content for which they are enrolled In fact I am sure that the greatest number of our faculty have acted ethically in every instance However, in no way can we condone the use of classrooms to discuss negotiations except in the limited instances where collective bargaining may be an item of predetermined course content I have no doubt that you would agree with this posture

A second portion of the student petition requests a letter of standing" on negotiations from the Board point of view In our efforts to conduct negotiations as a viable through a chief negotiator rather than in the media or among students we have avoided ten much public disclosure in early stages since we feel this can hamper progress and reflect negatively on both parties We are reluctant, therefore to respond to this request with a full "point of view" document however we are preparing a brief status report for release to the students which will hopefully answer some of their request

?? af

they

since t h e y began,
new leaves have been borne
  on the trees of the fields.
the leaves have grown large
  - and a deep lush green.
now it is fall!

you may be hoping that the leaves
  will now all turn yellow.
i suggest to you,
  that the leaves this fall
  may very well turn
    - very red
    - a very angry red.

        - A. F. Tunion (pseudonym)

Roach Reviews
    "Last Tango in Paris"

By TOM ROACH

With all the publicity that this film has had I
doubt if anybody will go to see it expecting a
documentary on the dancing situation in
France's capital. More than likely people will go
to see it expecting another professional stag
film, possibly on the order of Deep Throat or
Curious Yellow In either case, the dance freak
and the hard-core pornography fan will be
equally disappointed. Not that there isn't a lot of
sex and a little dancing involved in it, there is,
but because what Last Tango is concerned with is
found mainly in the dialogue and the characters.

It has been said that Brando plays a different
type of roll in this film. I would have to disagree
with that, in a very basic sense this is still the old
Brando. He is just as impulsively irrational as he
was in Street Car and The Wild One, and most
importantly, he still wields that charismatic attitude of masculine illusiveness that coupled
with the revealed inner core of a hurt, scared little boy, have made his career as an actor. Rather
than a break from the usual , this new role gives
Brando the opportunity to use his talents in a
dramatic tour de force that rivals anything he
has done to this date.

It would be wrong to assume that Brando is what
makes this film a success, though. Certainly
much of its phenomenal box office draw can be
credited to him but the fact that Last Tango is an
interesting and well done artistic achievement in
the field of movie-making can only be attributed
to everyone who had a hand in creating it. With
its flawless presentation of a soul searching
script about a desperate, guilt-ridden man who
hides from reality while at the same time con-
fronting it aggressively, intwined with an impressive concept that takes dialogue, music and
action on an equal basis and fuses them into pure
mood, and its refreshingly straight-forward attitude toward sex, Last Tango in Paris is a
powerful new force in film-making that over-
takes Brando's own striking performance to
become a unified landmark in its field.

What's so refreshing about a sex scene? Only
this. Practically every time one gets inserted
into a movie, one of two things happens; either it
is exploited to the point of being laughable, or it
is handled in such a cautious, artistic fashion
that it becomes equally absurd. Tango makes no
attempt to do anything with sex except us it point
blank to support its plot. The result is a mature,

tastefully hard-core approach, that after all the
trash that the industry has subjected us to, I
didn't think was possible; and that is refreshing.

As for the sex kitten who plays opposite Brando,
I simply can't recall her name. However, I'll
never forget her blue jeans.

the year in the nation was eventful .... women's libbers howled with glee as billie jean took
riggs to task ... the year at jrco was just as eventful .....

NEW PRESSURES ON NIXON

ELLSBERG CASE: FORMER NIXON AIDES INDICT[...]

ONE MORE SURPRISE IN THE WATERGATE CASE

THE GREAT TRUCK BLOCKADE

FROM RANCH TO TABLE— WHY BEEF COMES HIGH

AGNEW: "I HAVE BEEN DESTROYED"

Vice President Ford is sworn in at the Capitol

WHY THE CRAZE FOR THE "GOOD OLD DAYS"

16

LATEST UPHEAVAL IN GREECE: ITS MEANING TO U.S.

HOW KOHOUTEK WILL LIGHT THE HEAVENS

PRESIDENT REITERATES: NO PRIOR KNOWLEDGE OF WATERGATE BREAK-IN; TOOK NO PART IN NOR WAS AWARE OF ANY COVER-UP

Americans may get answers to some crucial questions soon-er than most expected.
The tempo is picking up—in both courts and Congress.

WHERE THE INVESTIGATION STARTED BY ARCHIBALD COX STANDS NOW

IF THOSE ROAD SIGNS PUZZLE YOU—

The Veep Most Likely to Succeed?

THE "GOOD OLD DAYS"

Cleveland
124 MILES
200 KILOMETERS

AND IN ARGENTINA—
Ex-Dictator Regains Power

WHAT MITCHELL AND DEAN SAID ABOUT THEIR TALKS WITH THE PRESIDENT

the year's events at juco were darkened by the problems involved in negotiations. . . .
.teachers were forced to strike and students gathered to hear administrative and faculty
opinions. . . . .

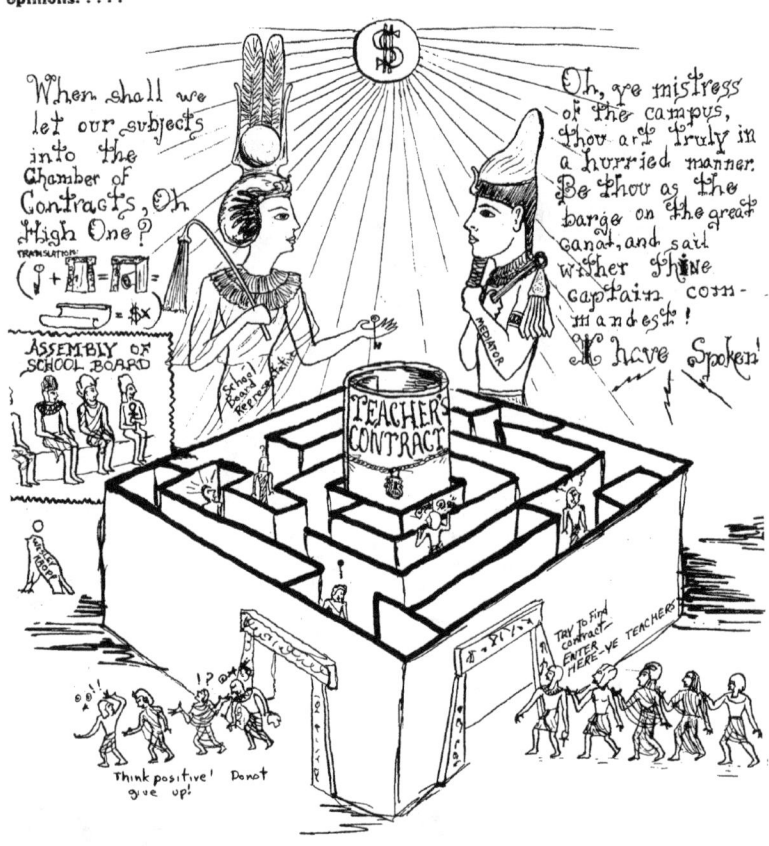

B. WEBB

a word association trip
            - w. h. watling

it was dusk:

      cool, shadowed and growing dark.
linda was driving:
      the car lazily followed
the lines on the road
through many turns,
continually escaping
to newer sights.
she was tired:
      yet awake;
the rest of sleep
was miles away:
      at length,
in the distance
she saw a shape:
      from its form and attitude
she thought it was an animal,
and as she looked more closely
she noticed there were several.
standing in the grass
along the edge of the field,
it seemed they were cattle:
      so freely and gently they grazed
she knew it was a herd of two,
a handsome bull and lovely cow.
but there was something else.
between us and them
there were weeds:
      a pesty grass
that grows thick

and makes a mess
of the neatest garden
(even a dreamed one)
when it swamps
the eyes with distortions:
      hazy and uncertain,
ugly and deceiving mutat
this the weeds had done,
for as we drove
up close to them
we could see more clearly
what we had taken for
a pair of happy cattle.
they were both fencepost:
      mere sticks lacking p
planted along the ditches
of a country road.
it had only been
the tall weeds around the
that had cruelly warped
from seeing a fenced-in p
      with a yardful of thi
a huge, fast and hollow c
and a generous share
of other greedy little mo
            ****
later, on a curve in the r
the car lights cut
undistorted through the c
to strike a wolf:
      a skinny, scrawny,
vengeful-looking scaveng
that looked at us
as though it would attack
and then was gone.

homecoming . . . . fall festival . . . . 1974 . . . . scenemakers . . . .wolves 21/rock valley 31

one of the social events of the fall season . . . . . . floats, dance, game, parade . . . . people, fun
. . . . royalty . . . . queen lynn marry and king john maier . . .

24

HOMECOMING '73

Bill Flint
Ski Club

Judy Bronson
Letterman's Club

Rogeria Powell
Brosis

Charles Graves
Brosis

John Popek
Letterman's Club

Diane Stampar
Teachers' Club

Diane Drick
Press Club

Bill Watling
Press Club

Sherri Porter
Engineer's Club

SATURDAY, OCTOBER 13

Steve Mahoney
Teachers' Club

John Maier
Chess Club

Maribeth Edwards
Chess Club

Patty Mozina
Nursing Club

Lynn Marry
Student Ag Assoc.

Ken Redfern
Student Ag Assoc.

Pat Augustyn
Epicurean Club

Andrea Grant
Epicurean Club

Jeanette Hanneken
Ski Club

theatre . . . .theatre . . . .theatre . . . .theatre
. . . .theatre . . . . theatre . . .madwoman of chaillot
. . . . march of '73 . . . . jeager, mc quilien, rogers
. . . .director mallary . . . .gold . . . .oil . . . .smashing
performance . . . .

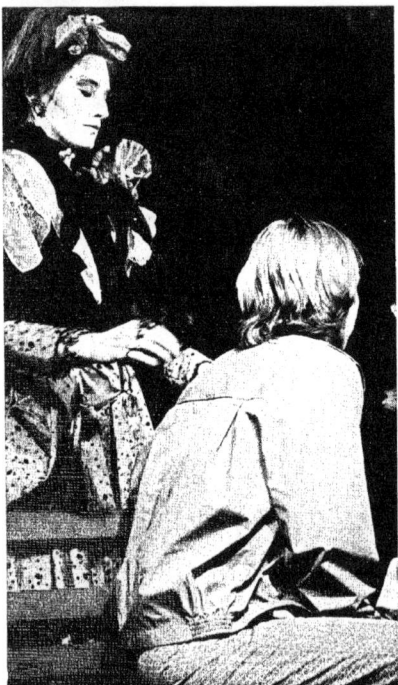

"Butterflies are Free"

One of the most valuable experiences that any of us can get from college is the non-professional entertainment that we, as students, offer one another. Admittedly, these experiences aren't as numerous or elaborate as they might be at a four year college with more financial encouragement and a larger enrollment, but perhaps it is these problems that make what we finally do produce here that much more valuable because we overcome them. We have art displays, music recitals, a literary magazine and less frequently, but most impressively, the plays and musicals presented throughout the year by the J. C. Players.

"Butterflies Are Free", their first production this year, was a smooth and successful study of two characters, Don Baker and Jill Tanner. The plot of this 3-act play revolves around Don's struggle to free himself from an over-protective mother and gain his independence as an individual. Keeping Don from making his break is the fact that he is blind and lacks self-confidence. From the blindness to the self doubts, Tom Reeves plays Don Baker with professional ease.

Don might never have escaped the death grips of motherhood if he hadn't met Jill, the flighty girl next door. She is full of hangups herself, yet capable of seeing into Don's problems and giving him the advice that he needs. Jill is played by Cindy Seng, who of the three major characters, has the least experience and comes across the most memorable.

My favorite part of the play was probably the least important. It came when Don and Jill were alone in the first scene. They were just talking, but it was so natural that the actors could no longer be distinguished from their roles. The play disappeared and it was only the three of us in the living room (Tom, Cindy and me). I refrained from involving myself in the conversation, however, because somehow I knew that if I did, Mrs. Stone would never give me another front row seat.

The actual highlights of "Butterflies" were when Jill stood up to Mrs. Baker, when Mrs. Baker decided she wasn't going to be Donny's crutch anymore and when Don and Jill, both suffocating in their own weaknesses, realize that they can help one another. Each one of these scenes calls for a change in the state of mind of the characters involved, and each one was successfully conveyed.

These were the hardest and the most crucial points in the play, and their polished, flawless conveyance can only be attributed to the hard work of the cast and a fine job of directing by Robert Mallary.

Juco's veteran actress, Peggy Granich, who played Mrs. Baker, was surprisingly effective in the role that was probably the hardest to identify with for a college-age actress playing opposite her peers. The relentless sarcasm, at times, laced the emphasis of a truly sceptical vicious attitude, but Mrs. Baker's domineering presence was definitely felt, body and soul, both on the stage and in the audience. The emotion charged scene where Peggy, as Mrs. Baker, exposes her inner self to Donny and they embrace rivals every other moment, including the climatic ending, for pure intensity and impact.

Then there was Ralph. Ralph is one of the weirdest people I have ever seen. There are only four characters in "Butterflies Are Free", but had there been forty, I am sure Ralph would have stood out. Don't get me wrong, Ralph was convincingly weird; I must admit that I left the theatre thinking that if I ever met another director of porno-plays he would be just like Ralph.

Ralph was played by Tom Smith. Your part was only on for a few minutes, Tom, what can I say? You certainly didn't have to say anything. You see, Tom, as Ralph does this unforgettable shiteatin' grin. If you don't like drama, you should have come to the play just to see it. Maybe if you missed it and you run into Tom in the halls and ask him really nice, he'll do it for you.

I have always felt fortunate to be able to write for a small community like JuCo and enjoy the communication and feedback that writers for papers with large circulations miss. For someone like myself and I know for the J. C. Players, this response is the only payoff. As I look through the

program, I count over fifty credits for people who contributed their time and energy to making "Butterflies" a success. I see only a few that I know - Tom, Paul, Art, Jackie, Lee and Sue. I wish I could name everyone, from the improved seating arrangement to the lighting and makeup. They all deserve congratulations for an excellent production.

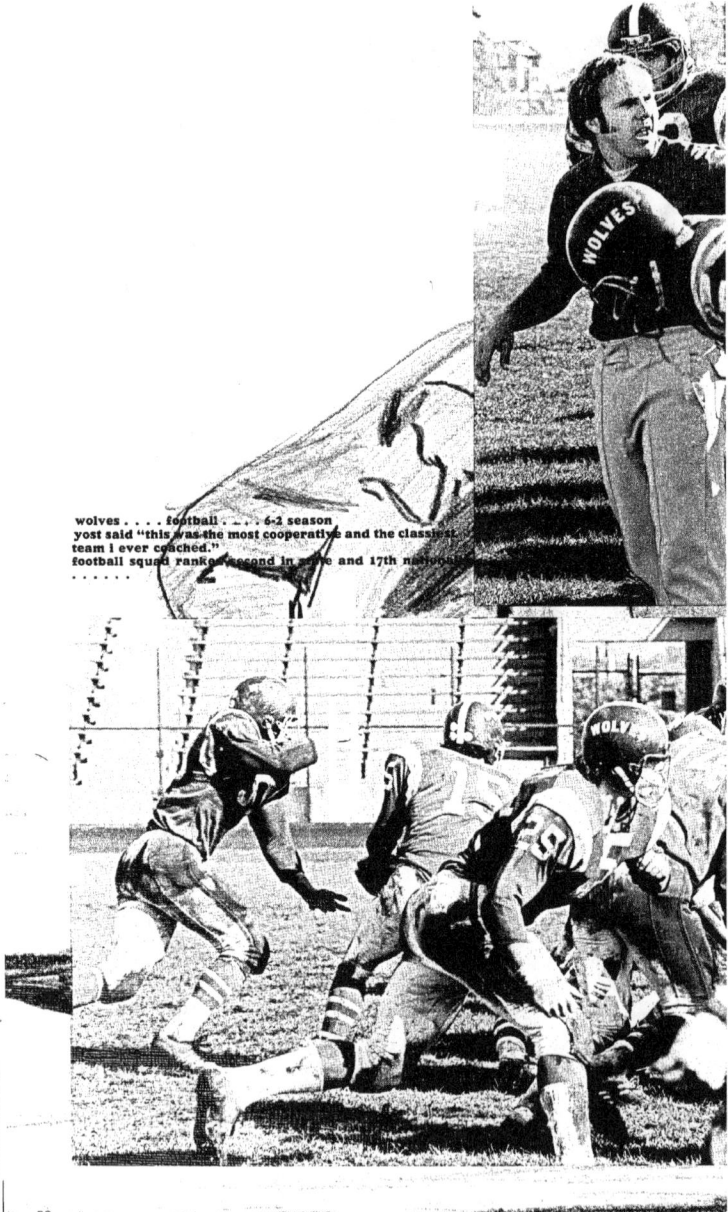

wolves . . . . football . . . . 6-2 season
yost said "this was the most cooperative and the classiest
team I ever coached."
football squad ranked second in state and 17th nationally
. . . . . .

this year's cross-country team under coach ivan
cooper finished the year with a record of 5 wins
and 12 losses. that may not sound too impressive
however, it's nothing short of a miracle that
ju.co. had a team. the year began with only 2
runners with 5 a must for competition in meets.
the year also started without a coach which also
is a must. so in order to shape a team a few minor
difficulties had to be overcome. these difficulties finally were overcome with six runners
on the team and mathematics teacher ivan
cooper being named coach.

the year overall was sort of a bummer with vic-
tories coming few and far between. a few of the
so-called highlights of the season according to
cooper were "i was pleased with the improve-
ment of the men over the season." he also expressed that "he was happy with having 6 steady
men towards the end of the season and that he
would like to compliment all the men who ran for
him."

in the region iv held at elgin community college
joliet placed 13th with a score of 297. top finisher
for the wolves was bruce reynolds who finished
23rd out of 109 with a time of 22:28 over a four
mile track.

the six men who finished the year for cooper
were bruce reynolds, bill steen, lee mcdonall,
dave larson, steve butler, and john parffrey. of
these six only reynolds and parffey are
sophomores so the prospects are much better for
next year than they were for this.

cross-country programs throughout the state
have been dropped by many junior colleges due
to lack of interest. lack of interest was the case
here at the beginning of the year, but thanks to
athletic director ken parker and cross-country
coach ivan cooper the program here at joliet
junior college is on the upswing.

The final club has been swung and this year's edition of Joliet Junior College's golf team has drawn to a close. Under Golf Coach Gil Bell the team finished with a 10 wins 5 loses record, in dual and quadrangular meets.

Some of the achievements of this year's team were: a third place finish in the N4C Conference, a third place finish in the sectional which qualified the team for the State Tournament and a 8th place finish in that tournament. Other highlights were a 10th place finish in the Danville Tournament and a 9th in the Joliet.

The individual achievements of this year's team were Fred Elhke 71, 2 under par at Lake County and Don Jennings 72 at Mayfair, in the Conference Tournament, Fred Elhke placed sixth with a 76 and Derk Beltzhoover ninth with a 77.

The team as a unit finished the year with 325 average, with the individual averages being: Fred Elhke a member of the All Conference team 79.9, Jerry Farber 82, Derk Beltzhoover 82.5, Don Jennings 82.5, and Steve Anderson 85.1. According to Gil Bell, Steve Anderson "Was the most improved golfer on the team over the last half of the season."

Prospects for next year are Anderson, Beltzhoover, Lanigan and Daley. So much can be looked forward to for the future.

Gil Bell said "he was quite pleased with the team efforts this year" and went on to say "that all his golf men played to their potential".

leadership conference . . . . fall 1973 . . . . lake geneva, wisconsin . . . . george williams college campus at lake geneva. . . . about sixty juco students gained valuable information concerning working with peers in leadership situations . . . . del kinney, director of continuing education at george williams conducted sessions . . . . organizations at juco sent reps to return with new ideas for the campus . . . .

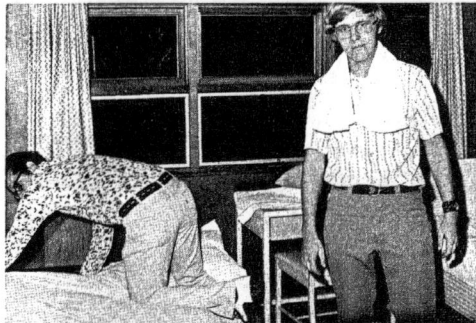

summer . . . . sunshine . . . . picnics . . . . sports . . . . rain, fall, football and publishing first issues of the paper . . . . juco hums throughout the year . . . people are the most important ingredient . . . . students, faculty, administration . . . .

people . . . . people . . . . people . . . . people . . . . people . . . .
people laughing . . . . playing . . . . eating . . . . working . . . . doing . . . . doing . . . . doing. . . . . juco at night and day . . . .

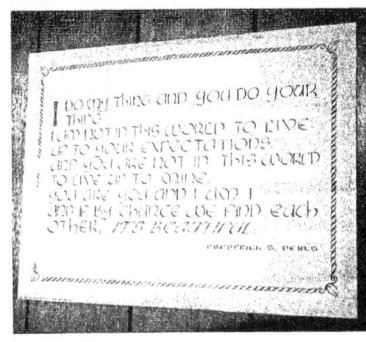

I DO MY THING AND YOU DO YOUR
THING.
I AM NOT IN THIS WORLD TO LIVE
UP TO YOUR EXPECTATIONS,
AND YOU ARE NOT IN THIS WORLD
TO LIVE UP TO MINE.
YOU ARE YOU AND I AM I,
AND IF BY CHANCE WE FIND EACH
OTHER, IT'S BEAUTIFUL.

FREDERICK S. PERLS

WORDEATER AWARDS
1972-73

ESSAYS
Best Movie Review - Tom Roach
Best Book Review - Tom Roach
Best Columnist - Tom Hooks
Best Campus News Story - Tom Roach
Best Campus News Story - Joan Hollister
Best Editorial - Gary Duncan

JOURNALISM
Outstanding editor - Carol Liptak
Outstanding photography - Dennis Trowbridge
Outstanding cartoonist - Jim Ridings
Outstanding Editorial Writer - Ed Bruske

Outstanding Reporter - Debbie
  Webster
Outstanding contribution through
  print media - Carlos Serrato
Outstanding Journalism Student -
  Mary Whitler

ART
Painting - Jim Laramer
Drawing - Margaret Schuster

3 Dimensional Design - Rondi Anderson
Pottery - Mike Vasquez and Kathy Baxa

MUSIC
Best Solo Performer - James Pozzi
Best Solo Performer - Melinda Mathews
Best Original Composition - Guy Shelley

VISUAL ARTS
Best Overall Movie - Rollin Gullata

FORENSICS
1st Persuasion - Frank De Loach
2nd Persuasion - Carol Bartz
3rd Persuasion - David Nolan
Oral Interpretation
1st - Peggy Granich
2nd - Mary Witt
3rd - Tom Reeves
Most Improved Speaker - Tom Reeves
Most Valuable Forensian - Carol Bartz
Best Speaker - Carol Bartz

FICTION
Best overall - Ed Verklan - "Dead Wait"
Best Male characterization - Carolyn Hunt -
  "Struggling"

Best Fantasy - Etha Griffin - "Windestate"
IN THE AREA OF SHORT POETRY
For Cleverness - Chuch Binkley "Your Cigarette Lighter Has Melted In Your Hand"
For Sound - Tom Partegys "Dry Beer"
For Narrative - Bruce McCallister - "I Hold Your Hair"
For Imagery - Robert Earley "Nightfall"
For An Overall Poem - Tom Partegys "Octagon"
IN THE AREA OF MID-LENGTH POETRY
For Imagery - Glenna Fox Fry - "My Mind"
For Sound - Bob Hatfield - "M'Butu"
For a Narrative - Robert Earley - "The Storm"
For Cleverness - Bruce McCallister - "Ripe Red World Factorial"

In Overall - Carolyn Hunt - "Awake at Night"

IN THE FIELD OF DRAMATIC WRITING
Most Serious Play - Joan Rogers
Most Comic Play - Charles Winan
For a Fantasy Play - Etha Griffin
IN THE AREA OF DRAMA
Memorable performance - There were 2 people chosen as major characters and 2 as minor
One-act play - Major character Mike Glester
Memorable performance
One-act play - Major character Debbie Jaeger
Memorable performance
One-act play - Minor character Tim Malloy
Memorable performance
One-act play - Minor character Linda Mock

juco plays host . . . . students work, play, reminisce
. . . . together

-harriet hardaway

Pastel Eyes

Look at the bricks
Between the cracks
In the wall.
Walk down a glowing sidewalk
And see dull oilstains on it,
Or walk on stains and watch
The glowing walk beneath them.
It's not death, it's the dying—
Looking back, before it's ended.

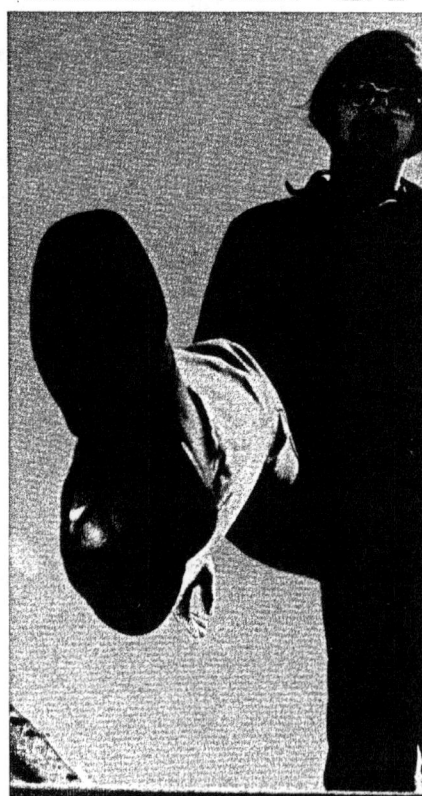

Walk by a tree
So frail and small
Suddenly to realize
It's just a blade of grass.
Stride over massive walls
On a spider's legs
Then race through vast accordion halls
At the speed of light.
It's not life, it's the living—
Look! Before it ends.

Whirl into a room,
Look back and see yourself
Come in three more times.
Place a candle in a bottle,
Watch it burst to a volcano
Dripping liquid fire.
It's not love, it's the loving—
Look into the fire!

In love with the door,
Not what's behind it.
In love with waiting,
Not the awaited.
Lying, burning, waiting
For the smash that never comes,
Soaking up love like a sponge
That was years in drying.

Pastel Eyes, Cont'd

Nothing new to see,
Only new eyes—
Prisms set with mirrored lenses,
Pastel eyes that see themselves,
Or the tongue that tastes itself
For the first time in its life.
             — w. h. watling, jr.

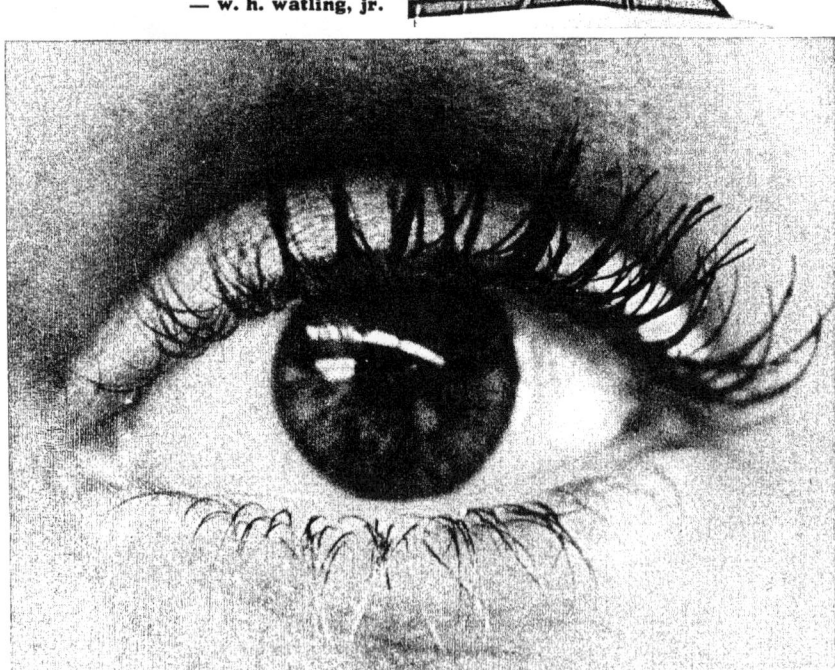

- jane hardaway

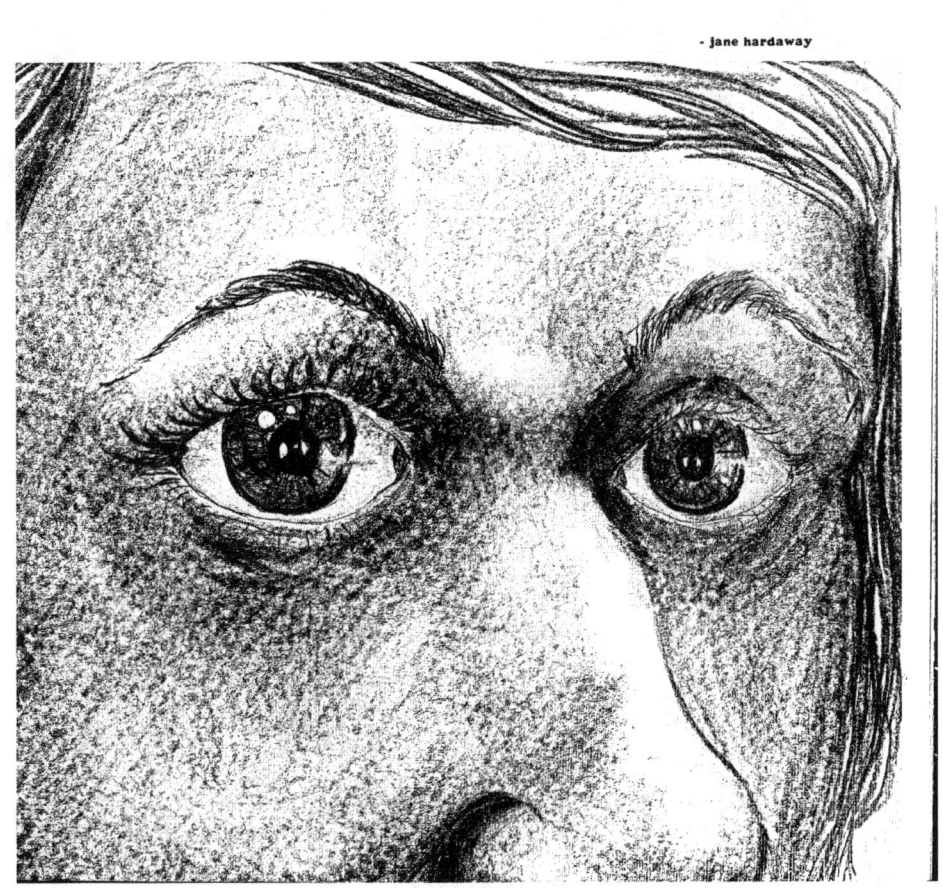

Students ... students ...

FALL SPORTS TO BEGIN SOON!!

Complete
Fall Sports Schedule

id mate in three

'isher Teaches

BE PRINTED
VEEK

Chess corner

White to move and mate in three moves.
(From "Bobby Fisher Teaches Chess")
ANSWER WILL BE PRINTED
NEXT WEEK

Chess corner

White to move and mate in th moves.
(From "Bobby Fisher Teac Chess")
ANSWER WILL BE PRINTEI
NEXT WEEK

In the months preceding and during the World Chess Championship Match of July 11 through September 1, 1972, the antics of Bobby Fischer were brought to worldwide attention. The American public was especially enraged and hostile toward him because of his threats to quit, his demands for more money and better playing conditions, his insistence on less noise, and his habit of showing up late for the first move. People wonder if all chess players act so strangely and why they do these weird things.

But chess players are different from other Americans and seem to hold Robert Fischer in great respect, believing that the things he does are not so strange. Chess is a consuming cancer that eats at one's insides. It drives the player to strive for perfection. A player's collection of books, magazines, clocks, boards, and chessmen is astounding. The number of memorized openings, traps, combinations, and end-game solutions is stupendous. And all this work for a game? Chess is more than a game. It is a study in human emotion (the opponent's and one's own) and in human response under pressure. Bobby's actions were the result of the intense pressures of master chess.

"Nearly all (great chess players) have had eccentric personalities—some to the point of mental illness."[1] Paul Morphy, an American who became world champion in 1858, suffered from paranoia. His history of disappointment and his final success in the conquest of the world championship reminds one of Robert Fischer. Each had difficulty in getting the incumbent champion to play him. After winning the crown, Morphy's delicate nervous condition worsened as he became afraid of being poisoned, only eating food that was prepared in the presence of his mother or sister. Wilhelm Steinitz (champion from 1866-1894) was schizophrenic and suffered from delusions that he could move chess pieces by electrical stimuli from his fingers and make telephone calls without wires or receivers.[2] Alexander Alekhine (1927-35, 1937-46) was a relentless, agressive player and has been called the sadist of the chess world.[3] He was a heavy drinker and was married five times, leading one to believe that he was a masochist too. He "once appeared at the Polish border and declared: 'I am Alekhine, chess champion of the world. I have a cat named Chess. I do not need a passport.'"[4] After losing games he sometimes threw his king across the room. Following the loss of at least one important game he smashed all the furniture in his hotel room.[5] Robert Fischer has been accused, among other things, of being afraid of women.[6] He has a history of walking out of tournaments. His eruptions and complaints of Russian collaboration helped force the International Chess Federation (FIDE) to change the rules of championship play so that a non-Russian had a chance to play the champion for the crown.

Lower rated[7] players exhibit all these characteristics and others as well. They develop strange antics during their games. A few dress flamboyantly wearing unusual hats, a necktie with dungarees, or a suit with just a T-shirt. Some experienced players use eccentric openings—for instance, the Baby Orangutan (an unusual left flank attack) and the Polish (a "Hog" attack that is horrid for about twenty moves but is harmless if the opponent survives), or defenses on the offense like the Pirc (a less aggressive flank opening), the King's Indian or Queens's Indian (off-center openings)—all of which are laughed at or treated in a most cursory way in chess books. Others smoke constantly, blowing smoke all over the place. Some announce that their opponents' king is under attack by a loudly stated "check" followed by a sadistic laugh.[8] A Chicago suburban housewife describes her strategy against males as "sitzfleish"; if she takes long enough between moves, 'her opponent becomes so annoyed and tired that he finally slips.'[9]

Between rounds in area chess tournaments players usually separate into groups. Card playing and eating do not usually become too rowdy, but others are not so quiet. Among the younger set football games are organized, basketballs might be rented from small kids for fifty cents per quarter hour, and bands might roam the town looking for signs of female life. At one tournament garbage cans were raided, milk cartons becoming weapons and large boxes becoming tanks. A forty-foot long window well became the "trench" to defend and a violent war game developed.[10]

The players are so "up" for their games that they do not stop after the tourney but carry their feelings inside them for a while. This mixing of chessboard logic with reality causes some strange reactions. One player lost his glasses on I-80 by hanging out the window of a car and screaming at a semi driver. Another had scars on his knuckles from punching brick walls and door frames after tournaments. At a party after a tournament one player seemed fine, but at one point he curled up in the middle of the floor and stared at the wall. He continued this through an ice cube fight and a tickle fight. Later he seemed normal again, but he remembers very little of the party. A fourth player showed signs of paranoia that developed from being paired against girls in tournaments. He found that he could not beat any girl with experience, and the two beginners that he did beat gave him much trouble. He developed a fear of girls and thought something ("The Plot") was after him. He thought all girls who were nice to him wanted to get serious, go steady, and get married. The thought of dating terrified him.[11]

Why do chess players do these strange things? Although each player has a different personality, when interviewed they all comment on the same type of reactions. During a game bodies become soaked with perspiration, and most players report substantial weight loss. Two players reported drops from 140-133 pounds and 180-170 pounds for a four round tournament. A chess clock[12] taken in for repairs was described as abused because of the force used to punch it after moves, an indication of the pressure of the moves. Notation, a very simple process of recording the game, is invariably messed up, no matter how careful one is in taking it. After a tournament many players describe their stomachs as twisted and their nerves as shot. A pocketful of antacids is essential. A common symptom is called "jelly brain"; the brain seems to wiggle and refuse to function. In this state a person is called "guished" because he feels as if he has been smashed by an irresistible force. Signs have been known to change before one's eyes on the way home, causing dangerous maneuvers in familiar roads. The chess board becomes life-sized and one's car, a bishop or knight with which to capture other cars.[13]

A study undertaken at Temple University recorded physiological parameters of eleven players rated 1300-1900. Diastolic blood pressure was up fifteen to sixty four percent over the resting state. Systolic blood pressure rose from a normal 120 millimeters of mercury to peaks ranging from 140-over 200 millimeters of mercury (the machine's limit). The heart beat had a momentary increase of between twenty and 120 percent over the resting rate. The breathing rate went from a normal four breaths per minute to a peak, for some, of over forty breaths per minute. The conclusions of the study were that "tournament chess playing does provide a reasonably good workout for some parts of the body" and that "those that tried the hardest (measured by motivation tests) had the largest changes, in general." This study "sheds light on elevated blood pressure experienced by both Mark Taimanov of the Soviet Union and Bent Larsen of Denmark during recent matches with our own Robert Fischer."[14]

Grandmaster chess players show many indications of the pressure of chess. In the Candidates Matches of 1971-1972 not only Larsen and Taimanov postponed games, but in the same series Heubner conceded his unfinished match with Petrosian, citing "nervous exhaustion".[15] In turn Petrosian postponed the seventh game with Fischer for "reasons of health." It was later hinted that his malady was also high blood pressure. While referring to the Candidates Matches of 1965, Boris Spassky describes the tension he felt when playing Tal as "a tense struggle." He continues, "There was no outlet for the tension. And the process of waiting for an outburst in one direction or another was simply unbearable."[16] These first two examples resulted from loses (6-0 and 6-0), Heubner drew six and then lost, and Spassky's description was of a

R., XXVI (September, 1971), pp. 493-495.

i would embrace you if i could
    -tom roach

i heard a sound at three o'clock
    awoke and followed it

            it led me to a window
            where pulling the curtain aside i could see,
            that there
            was no one there

it was only what i'd lost

        tapping a frozen branch

            against my window's frost.

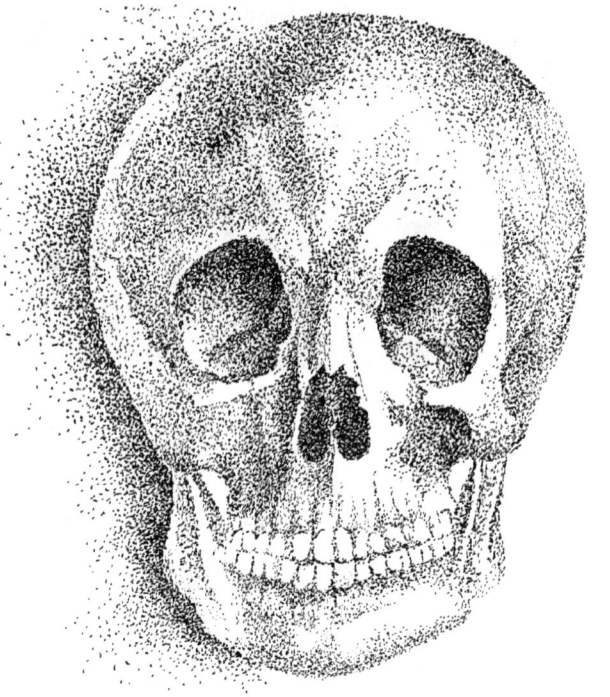

- sharon john, october 6

Oh, Marquis —

If you could see into my mind,
    it would scare you to death—
    sadistic things I think of
    with each and every breath.

Which way to drive my mother
    to a neurotic mess,
Or how to manage my night prowls
    to get one brother less.

Or how to squash our turtle
    or strangle the dear old dog
Or to tickle my sisters
    with a cute little twelve foot leg.

Yes, you may smile at me strangely
    and think I have quite a quirk
But I can say one thing for me—
    I'm happy in my work.
                    jac-lynn mc quillen

- janeane gradberg

The Secret That You Never Told

It's what made you do,
    What made you do, what made you
    do,
Whatever that you did.

It's the secret that is never told.
    That you tried so hard to share,
That departed with your soul

It's what you wanted so much to hide.
    But you, yourself, could never see.
You spent a lifetime keeping it inside.

It's the secret that,
    Was never heard,
Yet maybe understood.

It's your heaven,
    It's your hell,
Your ugliness and beauty too

It's your secret that was never told
    It's the secret,
That is you.

                    tom roach

Cagers See Great Season

Due mainly to very talented crop of incoming students a fantastic season could be in store. New students such as Pete Catchings, Phil Clarke, Forrest Harris, Gary Rauch, Bob Herrod to go with veterans Danny Robinson and Charlie Jones this school has a state power on its hands.

In the first three games total domination has not been the case, but rather lady luck has prevailed. The Joliet Junior College Thanksgiving Tournament was relocated to Elgin due to the teachers strike. This did not stop JuCo however from winning the Joliet at Elgin tournament. In the first game against Mayfair turnovers plagued the Wolves but we still prevailed 88-82. Charlie Jones led Joliet with 19 points. The Championship game held the following night Tuesday, November 20 against Elgin Community College finished with us topping Elgin 80-76 thus winning the tourney crown. Robert Herrod led Joliet's scoring with 19 points.

The home opener held November 27, is the type of game that could be called a thriller. The opposition Lake County lead most of the first half but Coach Tune switched to a zone defense the second half and this is what seemed to turn the tide. With .06 left in the game Lake County had the ball out at half court. The ball was taken out and played with too long and a desperation shot by L.C. did not even draw iron and JuCo won 69-68. High point man for us was Pete Catchings who finished the night with 20 points.

transfer day(s) sponsored by the counselors on campus provides opportunities for on-the-spot admission to the various four-year institutions represented at juco on these various days. . . .students also find an opportunity to discuss admission requirements at other schools as well as investigating the curricular offered elsewhere. . . . . .

nostalgia .... nostalgia

nostalgia .... the word for 1973-74 ..... kingston mines theatre opened its production of 'grease' (a nostalgiac look at the late '50's and early '60s) .... fashion designers revived the 'old' looks ..... record companies made a mint as they brought back the tunes popular with the 'young crowds' of a decade and a half ago ...... film companies introduced 'american graffitti' and students of the '70's relived moments that made the 'older generation' sigh as it remembered. the faculty at juco can remember well some of the moments that have been brought back on film, television and radio ...... here they are as they lived through those 'good old days'.................

frank alberico, virginia allen, bill allen, pat asher, gil bell, ed beltzhoover, grace brewer, bill brinkman, bob burke, bill burns, maurice cameron, paul carter, bill chase, margaret cockbill, duane converse, john corradetti, bob cottingham, bill curry, hal dellinger, jim egly, si ellingson, don esworthy, jim genseal, lee gould, dick harder, ed hassler, earl henslee (on sabbatical), john hirmer, len hodgman, jim hurst, georgina johnson, paul johnson, bill johnson, bob jurgens, bill kahle, sharlene kassiday, pryce keagle, stan kosiba, bill krause, earl kurtz, max kuster, neil lance, mel larson, steve lenich, paul lester, myra linden, bobby mc dowell, bob mallary, natalie miller, dick meyers, wilbur miner, pete neff, everett nelson, gil nicoll, fred norlin, ken parker, jake pottgen, jack richardson, manuel rodas, bev shields, helmut sienknecht, bob sterling, john stobart, roz stone, mary taylor, ted thompson (on sabbatical), lloyd tinkle, bob truitt, marty vanko, dean van tassel, georgia whitley, sandra winslow, bob wolz, art wagner, art walters, ken warman, charlie warthen, jerry yost, bill zales.

n
o
s
t
a
l
g
i
a
.....nostalgia

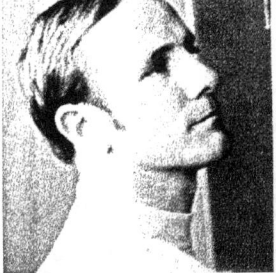

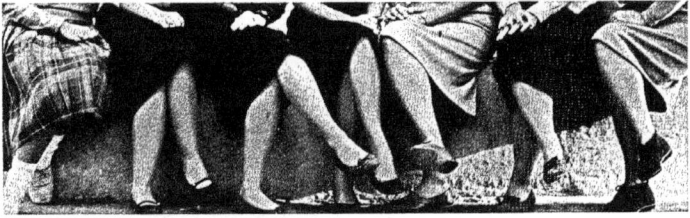

Janet
SHARPE

- janet sharpe

sga .... student government association .....
elected tom roach as president during october
... attended leadership conference ..... dean
rousenelios and joanne hollister served as vice
presidents .... joye woodhead filled secretary's
position ...... christmas decorations filled the d-
mall ...... campus events were coordinated by
members of sga .... roach presided at student
rally during teachers' strike......

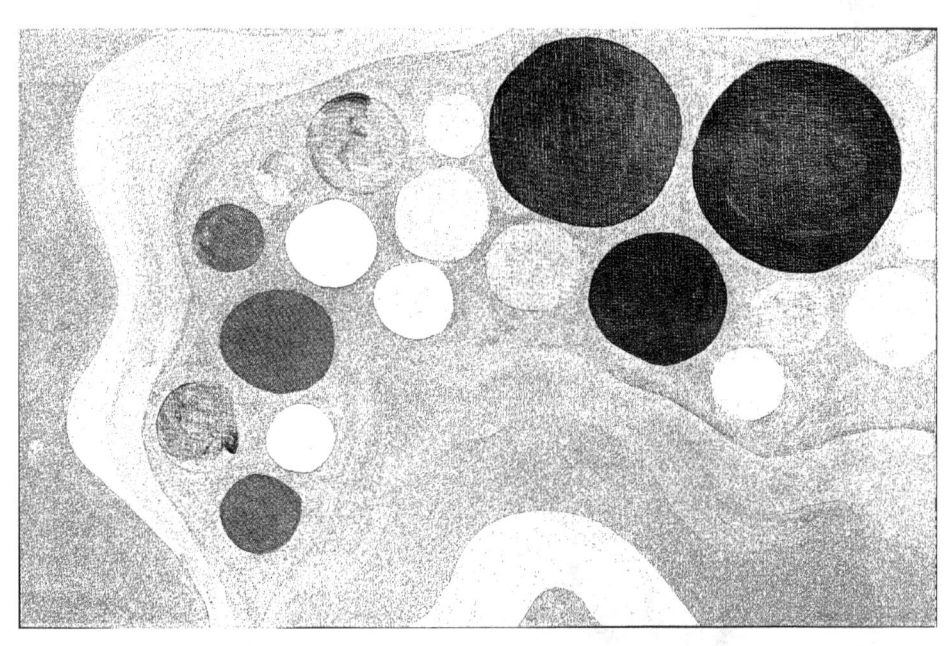

CABARET

directed
by
b. mallary
r. stone

Opening Night for "Cabaret" Thursday

An amateur production of the hit musical "Cabaret" is scheduled for December 6, 7 and 8 at 8:00 p.m. and for December 9 at 2:00 p.m. in the theatre at Joliet Junior College.

Members of the JJC Players involved in the production have extensive drama experience, during high school, at JJC, and with the Curbside Theatre and the Tangerine Tent.

Several of the lead roles are played by theatre majors at the college. These include Mark Selfridge who plays the American journalist, Bill Greene who plays Herr Schultz, and Sue Hatzis who plays Sally Bowles. (Miss Hatzis' major is music, but future plans include a possible careers as professional dancer and singer.)

Mark Bostjancic, who observers say plays a superlative Emcee in the production, is torn between the desire to teach voice and biology.

Students in the production graduated from virtually every high school in the district.

The choreography for the production is under the direction of Fran Fredericks, well-known Joliet dance instructor.

The musical is being directed by Rosaline Stone and Robert Mallary, sponsors of the JJC Players.

According to Ms. Stone, the musical is an excellent showcase for the many talents of the students. "Those who have seen 'Cabaret' know that it involves the whole gamut of acting abilities from comedy to pathos as well as extensive musical presentation," Ms. Stone said, "We believe that our students combine an acme of talents in the production."

She recommended that seats be reserved well in advance to assure admission to the production.

Admission is free to anyone with JJC I.D. cards. Other students will be admitted for a $1.00 donation upon presentation of student I.D.'s and others will donate $2.00.

CABARET
Cast in order of appearance

Master of Ceremonies (Emcee) Mark Bostjancic
Clifford Bradshaw . . . . Mark Selfridge
Ernst Ludwig . . . . Pete Graham
Customs Officer . . . . Burt Collins
Fraulein Schneider . . . . Mary Witt
Fraulein Kost . . . . Diane Forbes
Herr Schultz . . . . Bill Greene
Girl on the Telephone . . . . Jac-Lynn McQuillen
Sally Bowles . . . . Sue Hatzis
Sexy Lady No. 1 . . . . Toni Tweedle
Sexy Lady No. 2 . . . . Sandy Spivey
German Sailor No. 1 . . . . Jim Costello
           No. 2 . . . . Paul Rittof
           No. 3 . . . . Tom Reeves
Taxi Man . . . . Jim Loukas
Max . . . . George O'Kain
Nazi No. 1 . . . . Joe Hardaway
Nazi No. 2 . . . . John Parffrey
Waiters . . . . John Parffrey
                         Omar Periu
                         Mike Kerr

MALE CHORUS
John Parffrey
Omar Periu
Mike Kerr
Tom Reeves
Thom Smith
Don Shepherd
Burt Collins
Jim Costello
Paul Rittof

FEMALE CHORUS
Mary Ann Governale
Luanne Scholtes
Louise Converse
Linda Johnson
Sue Mitchell
Sharon Gonda
Deb Jaeger
Diane Bruske
Lee Roach
Joyce Slocum
Sandy Spivey
Toni Tweedle

PRODUCERS

Directors . . . . Rosaline Stone
                                  Robert Mallary
Technical Director . . . . Robert Mallary
Assistant to the Directors   Toni Tweedle
Choreographer . . . . Fran Fredericks
Band Preparation . . . . Jerry Lewis
Voice Coach . . . . Helmut Sienknecht
Musicians:
   Pianists . . . . Bev Nordstrom
                               Sylvia Forbes
   Percussion . . . . Sergei Casper
   Bass . . . . Dave Fodor

Box Office	**Publicity**
Dave Zordan*	Ginger Yunker*
Bill Greene	Thom Smith*
David Foose	Bill Greene
Fay Fuller	Mike Kerr
Peg Granich	Terry Johnson
Costumes	**Hospitality**
Fay Fuller*	Mickey Moore*
Sandy Spivey	Fay Wray
Mark Selfridge	
Eves Costume Co.	
Kosacks Tuxedo Rentals	
	Make-Up
Lights	Cindy Seng*
Shirley Ludrovec*	Jac-Lynn McQuillen
	Cindy Getson
Properties	Claire Poole
Karen Haas*	
	Set
Sound	John Parffrey*
Jim Costello*	THE JC PLAYERS

89

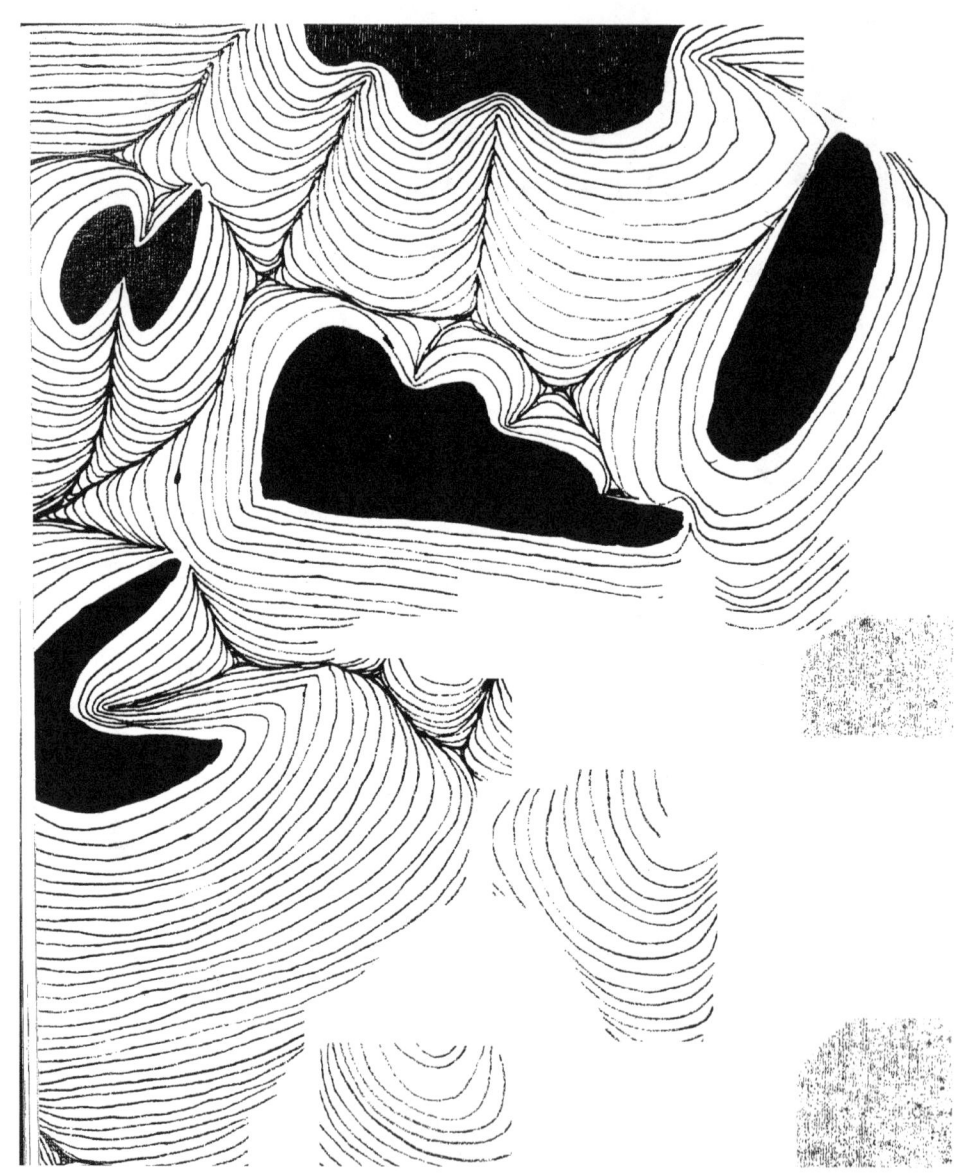

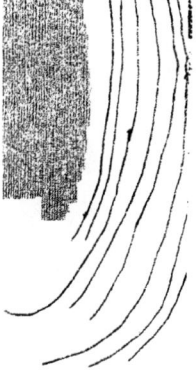

faces ..... people ...... working .... playing ......
thinking ..... relaxing ... relishing .... reflecting
..... people become the institution ..... the many
faces of juco are the many faces of those who
make the community of the junior college and
form an integral part of the larger community
.... laughing .... playing .... who are they? ....
what will they become? ......

to be continued

Vol. II

1974 shield
volume II
joliet junior college
joliet, illinois

volume II of the 1974 shield contains individual portraits of those students who had photos taken during the month of december, faculty candids, administration pictures, board photos, additional art work, original music composed in the jjc music department, more literature, sports and a myriad of photos reflecting the day to day life of jjc.

the shield staff for volume II: dennis trowbridge, w. h. watling, jr., cindy getson, kathy cook, liz higbee, bob vroegindewey. chief photographer for volume II was dennis trowbridge. adviser is bev shields.

wendell mc clintock

classes, socializing, working. . . .juco reflects a many-faceted life style as each day provides a myriad of experiences for all who will participate. . . .

abbott, laurie-frosh; achuff, edie-soph; akre, alan-frosh; aimberty, frances-frosh; anderson, carol-soph; anderson, mark-soph

anderson, shirley; archuleta, louisa-frosh; baletti, stella-frosh; bales, donna-frosh; baller, jacqueline-soph; beallis, cathy-soph

becker, aurelle-soph; bell, kim-soph; bennet,. brian-frosh; bergeson, delbert-frosh; bernhard, john-soph; beshoar, dan-frosh

besser, h. a. jr.-soph; beutel, karen-frosh; bingaman, pamela-soph; bjarnarson, nancy-soph; blackmon, barry-frosh; bode, george-frosh; bowers, marlise-soph; braccolino, sandra-soph; brehm, cheryl-frosh; brehm, dawn-frosh

brooks, delia-soph; brown, william-frosh; brown, marlene-frosh; brugnara, mike-soph; burke, joan-frosh; burrows, bev-soph; bustin, sue-frosh; cacia, angie-soph; carlson, nancy-soph; carnes, patricia-frosh

cartwright, kim-frosh; castaneda, evelyn-soph; chase, paul-soph; cleary, jean-soph; clower, patricia-soph; collofello, jim-soph

13

conley, kathleen; cook, kathy-soph; corneglio, don-frosh; cowley, greer-frosh; cox, jay-frosh; cramer, kathy-soph

creamean, bobbi-soph; cremeens, katherine-soph; creps, carol-soph; cripe, cynthia-soph; csepregi, tom-soph; d'amico, mark-frosh

dailey, steven-soph; davis, robin-soph; dial, linda-frosh; dipietrantonio, joanne; dooley, colleen-frosh; dooling, karen-soph

doran, carol-frosh; dotson, michael-soph; drick,
diane-soph; durkee, gail-soph; dzak, jim-soph;
dzuryak, cindy-soph; edwards, laurie-frosh;
edwards, maribeth-soph; ellis, bonnie-frosh; elwell,
carolyn-soph

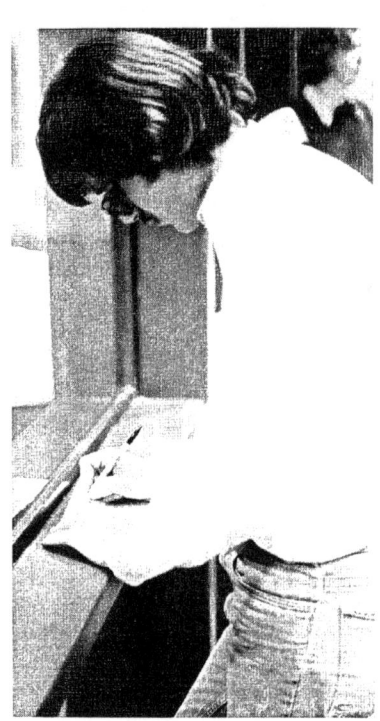

falk, eva-frosh; flink, betsy-soph; fitzpatrick, susan; foster, jeanne-frosh; gabel, mary-soph; geissler, ann; getson, cindy-soph; givens, valerie-frosh; goldasich, nancy-frosh; goode, carla-soph

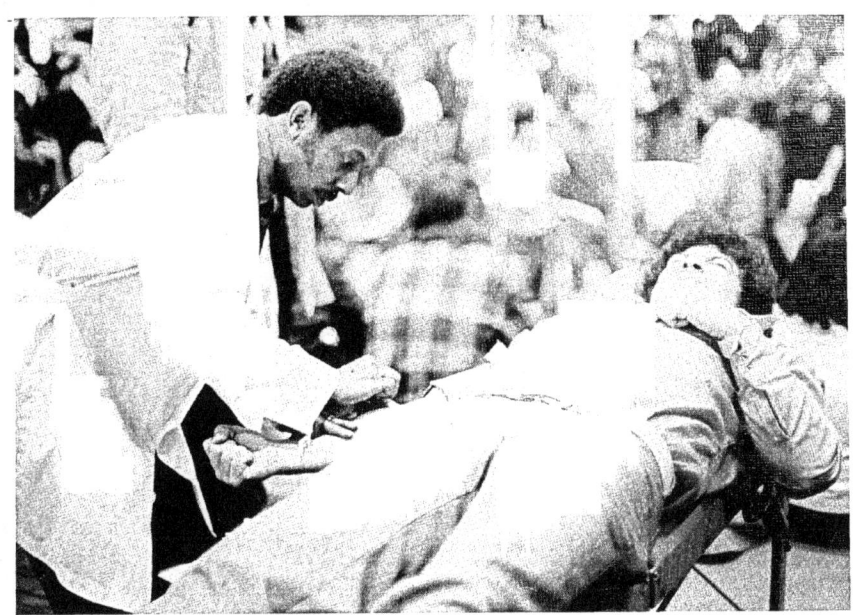

goodman, millie-frosh; governale, mary ann-soph;
grabavoy, marie-soph; grider, vickie-frosh; griffith,
david-frosh; guehler, gary-soph

guyer, linda-frosh; haas, karen-soph; haas, linda-frosh; hahn,
paul-soph; halterman, curt-soph; hancock, cecelia

hansen, brent-frosh; hardy, calvin-soph; harris, john-frosh; hartmann, john-soph; hartmann, laurie-frosh; hatzis, sue-soph; hedden, melissa-frosh

hennessy, debbie-soph; higbee, liz-soph; hiller, sherry-soph;
himes, bob-frosh; hinsketer, paul-frosh; hollister, joanne-soph

holmes, gary-soph; howaniec, janice-frosh; howland, michael-frosh; humi, dan-soph; hylik, debbie-frosh; ingmire, celia-frosh; jackson, cathy-frosh; jamnik, sue-soph; johnson, rosemary-soph; juban, sylvia-frosh

keenon, george-soph; keers, georgina-frosh; klein, rick-soph; knarr, marcia-frosh; knauer, john-frosh; kress, cathy-soph; kropp, wesley-soph; kucharz, paula-frosh; kulig, linda-soph; kuros, robin-soph

kuster, mark-soph; lance, betsy-soph; larson, dave-frosh; leonard, candice-soph; lestina, janette-soph; lestina, loralyn-soph

lewis, john-frosh; lexow, patti-soph; limbach, karola-frosh; lindstrom, mike-frosh; little, brian-frosh; livingston, larry-frosh

loukas, james-soph; lovell, joan-soph; lovera, diane-frosh;
ludrovel, shirley-soph; mackay, joanne-frosh; maier,
john-soph

marry, lynn-soph; marso, kathy ann-soph; martinez, ron-frosh;
matiak, carol-frosh; mauk, kathy-frosh; mccarl, rhonda-frosh

mcclure, ellen-frosh; mcclure, ronald-soph; mccullum, gertrude-soph; meagher, barbara-soph; michaud, greg-soph; miller, kay-soph; milton, celeste-soph; mitchell, susan-soph; moore, anita-soph; moore, mary-frosh

moore, mickey-soph; morgan, nancy-frosh; moss, john-soph; mozina, beverly-soph; mozina, patricia-soph; mulligan, elaine-frosh; mutz, cathy-soph; nemanich, judy-frosh; nemenski, phillip-soph; niestradt, robert-frosh

nordenberg, susan-soph; novy, julie ann-soph; oakley,
arlene-frosh; polmoari, gail-frosh; parker, dennis-soph;
peacock, cecelia-soph

peterson, carl-soph; peterson, michael-soph; pohl, gary-soph;
pullman, robert-frosh; racchini, joanne-soph; rathlisberger,
linda-soph

regan, sister kathleen; reynolds, bruce-soph; reynolds,
william-soph; rhodes, donald-frosh; riley, paul-soph;
risiile, sebastian-frosh

ritoff, paul-frosh; roach, tom-soph; roberts, cheryl-frohs; rose, cyndy-soph; rose, gary-soph; rousonelos, dean

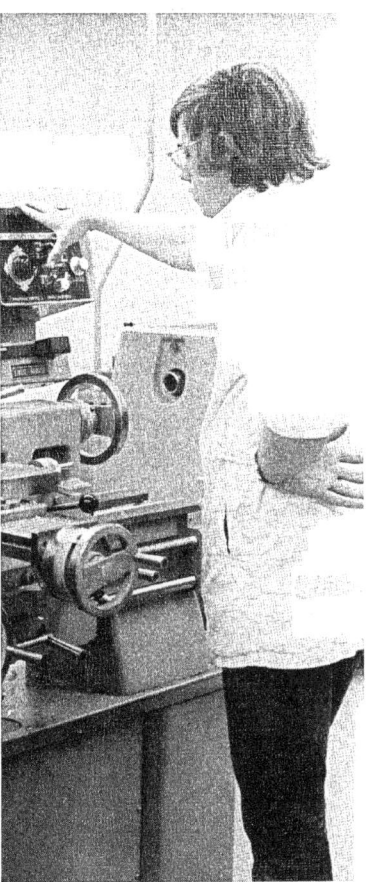

salemi, andy-frosh; sandretto, carol-soph; schmineke,
becky-frosh; schultz, susan; schuster, margie-soph;
semplinski, joyce-frosh; shelby, brenda-frosh;
sheridan, bruce-soph; shimer, janice-soph; skorupa,
kathy-frosh

slocum, joyce-frosh; spencer, lesley-frosh; spiezio, paul-soph; sponder, sheila-frosh; srygler, bob-soph; stefanich, sally-frosh; sterling, nancy-soph; stevenson, rita-soph; stewart, charles-frosh; stiglich, charlene-soph

stout, marianne-soph; sullivan, june-soph; swind, patricia-soph; synowie, linda-soph; tambling, alice-frosh; tanton, thomas-frosh

taral, jack-frosh; thomas, dale-soph; thomas, frances-soph;
tomala, joe-soph; turk, kathy-frosh; tyrell, jean-soph

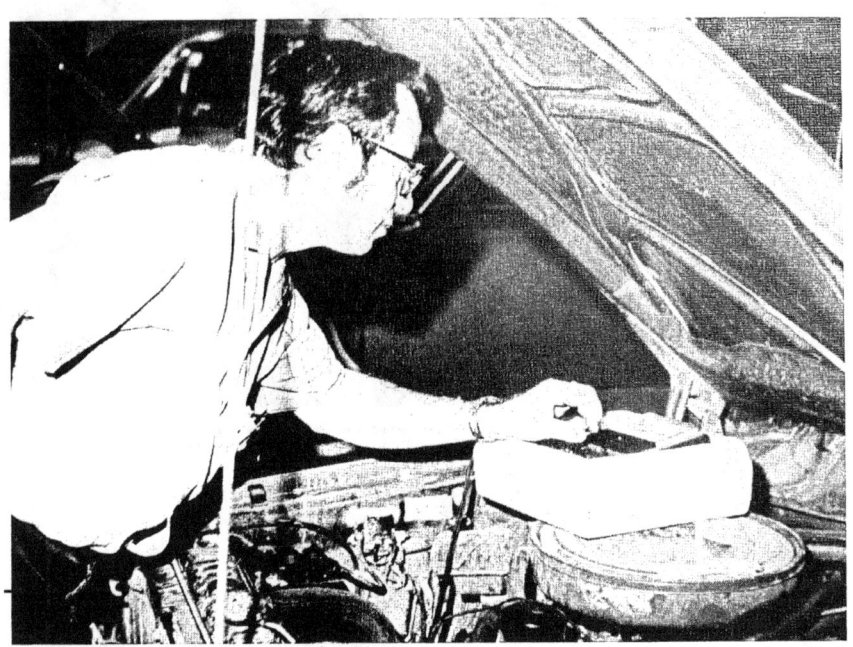

vantrease, william-frosh; vargo, sharon-frosh; vaughn, lynn-frosh; vaughn, randy-soph; vonch, linda-soph; vranich, pam-frosh

vreuis, susan-frosh; vroegindewey, bob-frosh; watling, w. h. jr.-soph; watters, judith-soph; weber, norma-soph; weigerding, jeffrey-frosh

wells, dale-soph; wendler, linda-soph; white, bill-soph; whitman, cheri-frosh; wicklein, clare-soph; wiersma, rich-soph; wilker, betty-soph; williams, connie-frosh; williams, jessie-frosh; williamson, peggy-soph

41

he **J.C. PLAYERS**
   Present
STUDENT DIRECTED ONE ACTS

UMB WRITER   Directed By
                               CINDY SENG

LIVE
SPELLED BACKWARDS

ected By   Directed By
INDA JOHNSON   MARY
                            GOVERNALE

J.B.

                8 PM
             APRIL 26-27
             J C THEATRE

DMISSION FREE

cast in order of appearance
frank ....paul rittof
the woman who knows almost everything (badly)
                                    diane forbes
richest girl in the world .... sue hatzis
the most famous playwright of our time ....
                                    al lentine
the best hustler in morocco ....w. james pohl
the most evil man in washington house ohio ......
                                    dan governale
cast in order of appearance
nickles .... larry kirin
zuss ....pete graham
j.b.................................... tom reeves
sarah .... sue mitchell
cast in order of appearance
gus ....burt collins
ben .... bill greene

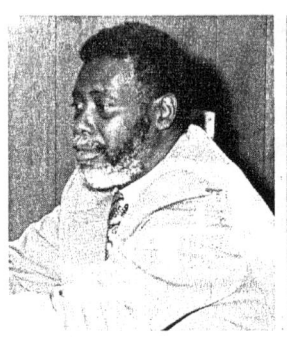

dr. h. d. mc aninch, president of joliet junior college. . . .served jjc during the '73-'74 school year in many capacities. . . .not only did dr. mc aninch fill the post of chief administrator at the college but also contributed time and effort to community causes among which were st. joseph hospital lay advisory board, joliet chamber of commerce, rotary club, board of directors for the united crusade. . . .dr. mc aninch's athletic interests were exhibited in the annual faculty-student volleyball competition. . . .in addition to the more strenuous activities, dr. mc aninch found time to assist the saa with its annual miss bikini contest judging. . . .guest lecturing in classes for various instructors consumed more time as did conducting faculty meetings and meetings with the board of trustees. . . .at the state level president mc aninch is on the board of directors for the illinois community college administration association and is a member of the finance committee of illinois council of public community college presidents and was recently named to the blue ribbon committee (finances) of the illinois community college board. . . .

45

administrative staff. . . .administrative
staff. . . .administrative staff. . . .ad-
ministrative staff. . . .administrative
staff. . . .administrative staff. . . .

executive dean
  of instruction .... dwight e. davis
dean of arts
  and sciences .... everett van de voort
dean of
  career education ....maynard boudreau
dean of student personnel
  services ....walter f. zaida
dean of community
  service (acting) .... jerome bradley
director of student affairs ..henry p. pillard
director of financial aids ...... donald tune
director of community
  relations ....doris slocum

dean of business ....james hines
associate dean of business ...robert e. glenn
director of admissions
  & records ....keith nanz
director of culinary arts .... claude kern
director of data processing ....ronald bleed
associate dean of student
  personnel services .... merron s. seron
director of research and
  planetarium .... douglas g. graham
manager jjc bookstore .... george miller

faculty. . . . faculty. . . . faculty . . . faculty . . . faculty . . . .represented by individuals holding advanced degrees from colleges and universities throughout the united states and europe the instructors at joliet junior college continually strive to provide the best possible for students enrolled in any curriculum. . . .thirteen departments form the foundation of the junior college's educational provisions and one hundred twenty faculty members endeavor each day to fulfill student expectations. . . .

alberico, frank p., public services; allen, virginia r., business education; allen, william t., biological sciences; anderson, mary ella, social sciences; asher, patrick, english

foreign language department chairmen, william i. burns, jr.; cameron, maurice, physical sciences; carter, h. paul, biological sciences; cattron, dave, agriculture

public service department chairmen, william chase; cockbill, margaret, english; converse, duane, physical sciences; cooper, i. james, mathematics; cottingham, robert, agriculture

business department chairmen, john corradetti; curry, william, social sciences; music department chairmen, hal d. dellinger; dugdale, james, art; egly, james, business education (on sabbatical)

mathematics department chairmen, e. t. silas ellingson; counseling coordinator, carolyn engers; esworthy, donald m., mathematics; counseling coordinator, roger gordon; gould, lee, business education harder, richard c., mathematics; hassler, ed, technical department; henslee, earl, biological sciences, (on sabbatical); heyen, robert, social sciences; hieggelke, curtis, physical science

hirmer, john, physical sciences; hodgman, leonard l., physical sciences; hurst, james w., social sciences; ingram, jean, counseling coordinator; johnson, georgina, public services

johnson, paul o., english; johnson, william bruce, agriculture; judson, r. louis, agriculture; jurgens, robert v., agriculture; kahle, william w., business education

art work by phyllis oudt

Kassiday, Sharlene, art; keagle, pryce, technical; kosiba, stanley, agriculture; krause, william e., music; krezinski, dan, physical science

58

lenich, steve, technical; lester, paul e., social sciences; lewis, jerry, music; linden, myra j., english; mallary, rogert a., english

manthei, dick, business; mcdowell, bobby, business education; meyers, richard, mathematics; miller, natalie, english; miner, wilbur a., physical sciences

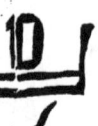

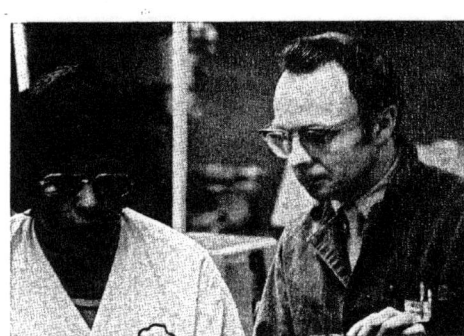

morris, james h., technical; neff, peter, english;
neisen, everett, biological sciences; nicoll, gilbert m.,
mathematics; nilles, louis j., technical

art work by cheryl profitt

61

norlin, frederick, c., english; o'connell, pat, public service; payne, joan, physical education; philip, arthur
w., technical; piket, philip, social sciences

art work by cheryl profitt

pottegen, jacob d., english; puddicombe, lula, librarian; counseling coordinator, alfred a. racchini; richardson, jack k., social sciences; rodas, manuel f., foreign language; parker, ken, director of athletics

schroeder, wayne, technical; schumaker, marvin w., librarian; shaw, betty l., biological sciences; shields, bev, journalism/english; sienknecht, helmut, (1928-1974) music

simmons, june, nursing education; solfronk, jacqueline, public services; social sciences department chairmen, robert e. sterling; stobart, john f., english; stober, siegfried, culinary arts; stone, rosaline b., english

taylor, mary, english; teater, david, business education; thompson, ted m., english (on sabbatical); tinkle, lloyd l., business education; truitt, robert a., physical sciences

vanko, martha, english; van tassel, r. dean, mathematics;
biological sciences department chairmen, arthur a.
wagner; walters, arthur l., foreign language; warman, t.
kenneth, public services

art work by cheryl profitt

9/30/73

rtment chairmen, charles warthen; weis,
s education; whitley, georgia l., nursing
slow, sandra j., english; wolford, james,

wolz, robert j., business education; yost, gerald, physical education; zales, william m., biological sciences; zabrocki, emily, director nursing education

mike dotson

anna duffles

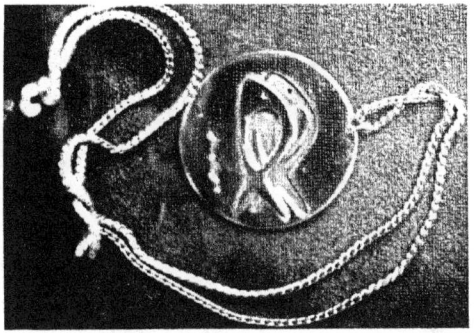

john ebert

tence is a slight-winged
y B that bumbles along,
ant of the impossibility of
ight.
nseen shapes only Become
le and moving to us when
are splashed by bright light
cles of C.
ould not See without, but
watch nothing except the
ow to all this, an organic
ra I.
Eye has given us a universe
ew. Yet would you fit your
ite debt to senses into
tiny O?
your jealous much-Owed
ue may well ask, "Do you
a P for me, or can you
at all?"
taste the Peas! Now grasp my
d know the upshot of this—
preciated as one sense may be,
also R.
you willing to take some
th every one, or abstain
letely from each party's
awhile?

Reject their Tea, and learn
what separates U from your
homonyms, archaic bowing shrubs and
sheep ruled by their sex.
Read no road signs. Instead, thirstily
push on, not caring how many
add up to a Y, or mark the
fork for You.
On the way to Why, you will
lose seven friends before
a time comes when you finally
have 1.
Your blistered feet will detract
seventy-eight miles until you have
Won, arriving at 2.
By then your lips, burnt from
voting down three times two thousand
poison oases, can only rasp this To
show at last you voted 4:
"I 8 not For days.
I 80 not in the desert.
But, tempted by your vastness
I 8000 at last,
I Ate Thou Sand at last."

Program for I-8000

by W. H. Watling, Jr.

71

the year in retrospect at joliet junior college provides students and faculty with reflections of a busy year. . . .a fun year. . . .a constructive year. . . .

nce Troupe Highlights Black History Week

by CAROL BROUGHAM

Junior College and other titutions participated in listory Week (February ith a variety of activities Black History week began on Sunday, Feb a trip to the Museum of History in Chicago The of St Francis sponsored e to the museum so area could view a presenta- "The Aesthetic Experi- he presentation included of black art from dancing g Cost of this trip was 75 person

ancis also-sponsored a out Dr Martin Luther r. . "Montgomery to '', and a dance following le Admission to this vhich was held at the all of St Francis is $1 00 sored black choirs from Illinois University and rdenominational Choir ., Missouri, on February e Interdenominational - a non-profit choir - been in existence for 15 ough all the members of are students at Lincoln

The Junior College also sponsored the Darlene Blackburn Danced Troupe, which performed on the D-mall of the permanent building at 11 00 a m and 1 00 p m , on the 15th, also The Troupe is a group of young dancers and drummers who presented the authentic dances of Africa as well as Afro-American variations of those dances for the education and entertainment of the audience. There was no admission for the performance of this dance troupe

A panel discussion was held on Wed , Feb 13 The panel consisting of Mary Anderson, history department, Doris Slocum, community relations, and Dr Elmer Wright, Associate Dean of Instruction, discussed the institutional racism

Lewis University of Lockport sponsored the Katherine Dunam Dancers on February 14 The dancers are from the Carbondale Campus of Southern Illinois University

The finale of black history week was a dance held at Lewis University on Saturday, February 16.

Wordeater Awards Announced

The Wordeater Awards for the first semester of the 1973-74 academic year have been announced by sponsor John Stobart. The winners and amount of cash they are to receive are as follows: W. H. Watling, $5; Earla Fowler, $5; Ginger Yunker, $5; Dave Zordan, $5; Patricia Harrison, $5; Charles Winans, $5; Barbara Strait, $5; Robin Davis, $5; Vickie Girder, $5; JoAnn Hauswold, $5; Joanne Hollister, $5. Winners of $10 awards are Glenna Ostenburg, Wayne Mooney, Jae-Lyn McQuillen, Linda Keith. Other award winners are Tom McCabe, $15; Tom Roach, $15; Etha Griffin, $15; Wesley Kropp, $20, Doug Emory, $20, and Bruce McCallister, $20.

JJC evaluated "... highly commended"

A recent evaluation by a team from the State Division of Vocational and Technical Education stated that "Joliet Junior College is to be commended for many of their program components which can be classified as exemplary."

The team, consisting of educators and businessmen from various colleges, high schools, businesses, and industries throughout Illinois, spent several days studying the vocations-technical programs at JJC. They particularly praised the "dedication of staff members of their programs and students, and the many efforts expended by staff members on behalf of the college and its service population without regard to reimbursement or personal gain." They also lauded what they called "the depth of understanding of occupational programs exhibited by the administrative staff."

The team recommended that the school improve services for and communications with part-time and evening students. A particular recommendation was that programs be provided so that a part-time student could obtain all requirements for a degree by taking only evening classes.

Another recommendation was that greater emphasis be placed on specific program articulation with area high schools.

The team concluded that "the programs offered are meeting community needs and are providing students with skills needed for employment. The district is to be highly commended for this commitment to quality occupational programs, and is deserving of the support given by the community, business and industry, and students."

Joliet J. C. Students ttend N.Y. Conference

loliet Junior College stu- irol Anderson, Paul Rit- oanne Hollister, attended York conference on the of November 9, 10 and 11. rence, entitled "The Col- on the student role in : bargaining." Sponsor- student senate of the City y of New York (CUNY), d workshops and speeches ts as well as lawyers, on ity and morality of stu- ng seated as a third par- ract negotiations between nd the Board of Trustees

'and administration.

Such a student is already a third party negotiator at Fitchburg College in Massachusetts. CUNY has also had a student representative at the negotiating table. In the negotiating student plays a role similar to that that the student board rep here will play; except JJC's student will not be present at the time of negotiations. Both play a representative student role, however.

There were approximately 80 people present, ranging from un- "dergraduate students, to graduate

students, to people working on their PhD.'s. There were lawyers, students, SGA sponsors, Board negotiators and school administrators. The wide variance in personalities led to interesting sessions all around.

Tapes of the conference, information provided by CUNY, and a written report by the three attending students will be available for students who are interested in Mr. Pillard's , office in Waubonsee Building.

jislators Visit Campus

lay, October 26, Joliet llege held "Legislative on Day" here on cam-

tion for students and leg- is held in the A-Building , from 10,50 until noon, okies and punch were all that attended. Among tors who attended were: nan O'Brien, Senator ator Mitchler, Shirley , Administrative assist- presentative Blair, Rep. invenweber, Rep. Sang- tep. Kempners and Rep. Rep. Beaupre, all of Ill- nislators talked on many

subjects predominate in the news today, from the regional transit authority to the Arab-Israeli War.

Approximately 100 students on campus that day ventured in to ask questions of the legislators. All the Senators and Representatives attended a luncheon here on campus from 12 00 to 1:30 P.M., also attended by the Board of Trustees, college Administrators, and Carol Anderson, Student Government Associating Acting President. After lunch, some of the senators and representatives took a tour of the campus; the others flew back to either their Springfield or Washington offices.

Veteran's Party deemed "Successful"

By CAROL ANDERSON

On Monday, February 11, the JJC Veteran's Club held its third party of this year The 18th Amendment, a nightclub in Shorewood, was the place for the event which featured Ziggy and the Zeu Revue, a nostalgic-style '50's band

According to John Thorsen, Executive Vice-President of the club, the party was a success Approximately 380 people attended the party, the proceeds of which will go toward a scholarship fund set up for Veterans "The reason we set up this scholarship fund is to help the veterans coming back to school," Thorsen said

Three parties have been held this year by the Vet's Club Besides the Valentine's Party, celebrations were held at Halloween and Christmas times of last semester They were also described as successful

The Veteran's Club membership is open to all, veterans and non-veterans "We could have more activities if we had more people," stated Thorsen The officers for this semester are Curt Halterman, president, John Thorsen, Executive Vice-president, Rick Turk, Public Relations Vice-president, Jim Marenchi, Communications Vice-president, Phil Shoemaker, Treasurer and Linda Spray, secretary Pat Asher is the organization's sponsor was reported shortly after 9 a.m. After lunch, more organized efforts took place.

Wearing ski-masks, neck ties, red sox and blue shoes two morning streakers raced through D-Mall to an awaiting get-away car in the visitors parking lot.

One said it was "pretty cold" and it was the quickest dash he ever made.

Shortly after 1 p.m. organized streaking started.

plain what the rationale was behind the event.

"It's against the formalities imposed by our society," he said. "It's saying we are not going to respect the taboos in our Western culture.

"Nudity is nothing in Asia. Here it's a big deal. There must be something wrong with us. We need an individualized identification."

Campus newspaper editor Joey Woodhead, 20, differed.

"They are not rebelling against anything," she laughed.

"It's just a fad. A welcome to spring. It's no different than swallowing goldfish, flagpole

Shortly after those words, two boys wearing nothing but one pair of wire-rimmed glasses made their dash to fame. And then eight boys wearing not even glasses trotted through. They made only one stop.

And that was to remove their jock-straps at the entrance of D-Mall.

Why did they streak?

A 20-year-old, talking in winded gasps but now wearing his blue-jeans "I don't know. It was on impulse. Someone called me chicken. I might do it again."

A 19-year old streaker added "Just for fun. I'll probably do it again Monday."

And a girl, after removing the red plastic sack to reveal dark

school regularly provides blood needed by 12-year-old Randy Hoffman of Joliet, a hemophilia victim.

"We decided to give a demonstration Friday to show how painless it was, but nobody came around, said Mrs. Slocum "Then all of a sudden streakers started coming from everywhere.

"Soon there was quite a crowd and we got down to business. Twelve persons gave one pint of blood each and 40 others made pledges."

The blood drive for Randy needs 300 pints a year.

(reprinted from March 9, JOLIET HERALD NEWS, with permission)

Press Club Members
Attend Conference

Seven members of the Joliet Junior College Press Club, along with 1,028 other students and 165 advisors from all over the nation, attended a three day conference sponsored by the Associated Collegiate Press (A.C.P.) from Thursday, November 1 until Saturday, November 3 at the Palmer House in Chicago, Illinois. Those students chosen from the Press Club to attend the conference with their advisor Beverly Shields were Diane Drick, Joanne Hollister,

Joye Woodhead, Paul Riley, Tom Roach, Dennis Trowbridge and Wesley Kropp.

The conference began on Thursday with registration, which lasted from 9:00 A.M. until 7:30 P.M. The opening convocation was given at 8:30 P.M. in the Grand Ball Room of the Palmer House by Dick Harwood, Assistant Managing Editor-National Affairs for the "Washington Post". The annual A.C.P. Pacemaker Awards were also pre-

sented to the six top college newspapers in the country. Various student - run rap sessions were then held immediately after the presentation of awards.

On Friday and Saturday, beginning at 9:00 A.M. on both days, the students attended numerous sessions which were geared to such aspects of publications as newspaper and yearbook production, newswriting, photography and advertising.

Political Science Classes
Plan Washington Trip

Ms. Mary Anderson, a Political Science instructor, has announced that an educational tour of Washington, D. C. has been planned by the political science classes for both political science students and other interested students. The group, who will be greeted upon arrival in Washington by a representative from Mr. O'Brien's office, will depart from Joliet on Wednesday, November 21 and will return on Sunday, November 26.

Highlights of the trip will be tours of the White House, Arlington Cemetery, various government

buildings and both Williamsburg and Jamestown, Virginia, where there are extensive exhibits.

The trip will cost $138.50 per person if a total of 45 students sign up to go. This fee includes first class accomodations at the Shoreham Americana Hotel, all major meals and entrance fees to Williamsburg and Jamestown.

Ms. Anderson describes this cultural tour as being " . . . a great chance to see the nation's capital and the very beginnings of American government."

Anyone interested in going on the trip is urged to see Ms. Anderson.

mike warrick

top to bottom . . . jack heffern, (left to right) ms. kremel,
marsha lega, cynthia rini

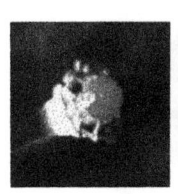 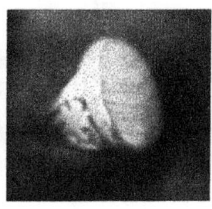 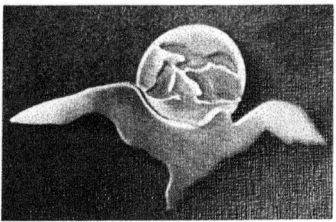

By DEAN ROUSONELOS

Student Government Association of Joliet Junior College has recently signed THREE DOG NIGHT, HEARTSFIELD, and ISIS for a concert appearance on March 16, 8:00 P.M., at Joliet Central High School Gym. The concert is being promoted and produced jointly by Joliet Junior College and Zoom Productions.

Three Dog Night, a world known contemporary music group, has piled up major hit after hit to their credit. Some of their successes include "One", "Eli's Coming", "Joy to the World", "Try a Little Tenderness", "liar", "Black and White", "Easy to be Hard", and "Shambala." All of their albums and singles have been consistently ranked at the top of the charts while they have been signed by ABC/Dunhill Records.

The group consists of three lead singers, Danny Hutton, Chuck Negron, and Cory Wells; Mike Allsup, lead guitar; Jimmy Greenspoon, organ; Jack Ryland, bass, and Floyd Sneed, drums. Three Dog Night has recently performed at Southern Illinois University and will be performing at Eastern Illinois University several days after the JJC concert.

Culinary Arts News

By LInDa GUYER

Students Keep Up With Growing Plant Demand

contented

Eagle manle in the sky
why is it that you can fly
and I must sit here below
envying your arial show?

You never seem to have a
care
soaring through the sky
so fair
Here on earth there is
such strafe,
someone takes another's
life
but you too must hurt and
kill
tearing flesh with claw
and bill
I guess your life is not
so great,
All of us give in to fate.
So be contented   I see
I must
All will die and turn to
dust
No matter if eagle or man
we must strive for all we
can
and be thankful for what
we've got
it's useless to try and
be something we're not

—bonnie J ellis

On: No

I·have seen
The ebbing tide
Edit another
Thousand grains of sand from
The beach, and drag them to sea.

I have felt
The tiny but
Persistent mite of
Time file off a few more
Cells that held part of my life.

I have smelled
The work of God—
A hungry crow tugging
The gut from a dead
Dog, leaving behind its soul.

I have heard
The agonized
Bark of an ocean
Crab tossed into boiling
Water for some fat man's dinner.

I have laughed
At geographers
Who try to trap worlds
While parting their nations
With a flimsy net of ink
And numbers, one to ten.

I have known
Those who lure to
Rule, and their mood of
Doom. I repel like a
Leper their toy iota
Of planetary power.

I have cried
Over raw corpses
Of war— men who once
Slept snugly with guns, whose
Body sap I have seen pass
Bubbling through charred, barky limbs.

I have screamed
That sad will end
Any knave so vain
To think that he can snare
Pure rains in the gory slit
That a bomb blast tills.

I have not
Been pleased to watch
And weep upon some pew.
No prayer on Saint Luck's
Faithless skull can make parks
Spring from human scrap.

I have tried
To find the door
To a new road, beyond
The loveless wall of law,
That could lead us up from
The ooze of this flesh-eating zoo.

I have dared
Spill from my lips
A Call to other lambs
Of this frightened herd
To skirt the tricks of those
Who mire the earth in rimes of death.

I have begged
Those tired of being
Sacrificed, no more
To fall into mute tombs,
But to shout a steady, "No!"
And smite and not be smitten
By the tides of their own times.

                              -w. h. watling

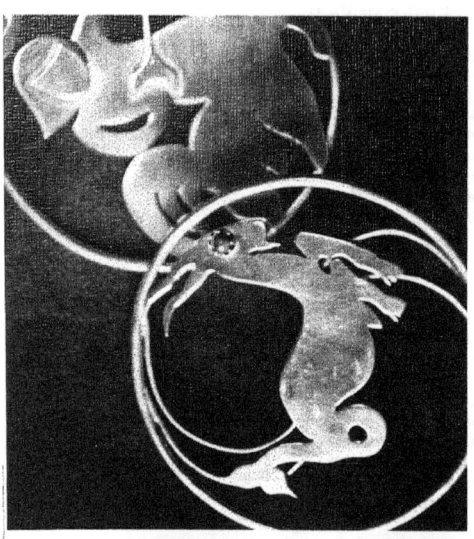

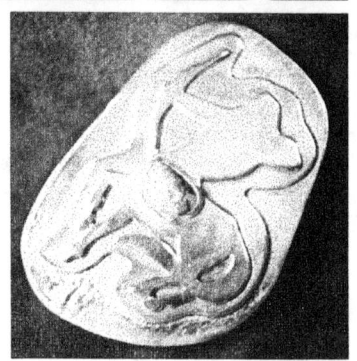

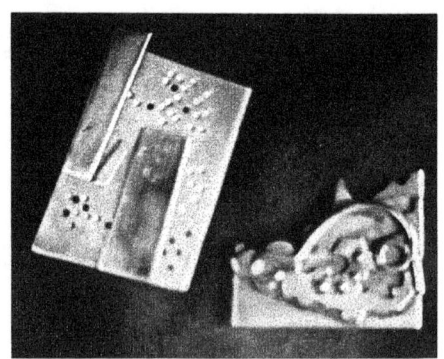

top to bottom, left to right, art work in jewelry by: mr. and ms. kremel, steve brooks, jack pepper, marsha lega.

a percussion choir
for nine players

by david fodor, 1974

continued on page 81

continued from p. 80

continued on p. 88

81

grapplers seize national rating. . . .send 7 to minnesota. . . .

Pillard's Men 10th Nationally

A pre-season survey of NJCAA wrestling coaches has placed Joliet Junior College's matmen in a tie for tenth place nationally in early season thinking. The JJC team is the only Illinois team to make the top ratings, although Forest Park Community College, Harper College, Lakeland Community College, and Triton were mentioned for national ranking.

The survey indicates that defending 1973 champion North Iowa Area Community College is figured to make a strong bid to repeat, with Farmingdale Agricultural and Technical College of Farmingdale, New York figured to made another strong showing.

According to Coach Henry Pillard, this year's Joliet Junior College wrestlers include some fine men who "may very well make a name for themselves and for the team on a national basis."

Nationals this year will be held at Worthington, Minnesota, February 28 through March 4. Joliet will be represented by seven men. Matt Boyle (118), Bill Hayes (150), Joe Tomola (158), Brad Day (167) (not pictured), Steve Brandt (177), Randy Dockstader (190) and Heavyweight Mike Kettman.

To qualify for this tenacious tournament our Wolves had to place either 1st, 2nd, or 3rd in their respective weight classes at the State Regional held at Blackhawk College. We had no champions but did finish with six second place finishers and one third place finish. The team totals at Regionals were Blackhawk 117 points, Harper 109½ points, and J.J.C. 107½ points. It's surprising we did as well as we did. Mr. Allen, assistant coach commented that the tourney was dominated by sophomores. Our team is

basically freshmen and this has too add optimism to our coaches.

It should also be noted that we ended the Dual-team season ranked 5th in the nation.

A review of the season indicated many highlights. At 118 Matt Boyle finished the season with 19 wins and 1 loss and has qualified for national after taking second in the state regional.

Eugene White at 126 was very impressive all year, taking second at the University of Illinois Invitational and was M.V.P. at the Madison Tech Invitational. Eugene did not qualify for the nationals because he did not make weight for Regional competition. He is a fine wrestler and will undoubtedly be a strong contender next year.

Bill Hayes at 150 has had an up and down year, but still managed to qualify for the nationals by taking second in the regionals.

At 158 Joe Tomola has been very strong and consistent. He also will be headed to Nationals after taking a second at regional. Brad Day (not pictured) at 167 was champion at Richland Invitational and will also represent Joliet at the Nationals. Steve Brandt, now wrestling at 177 placed second at the regionals and will be a strong contender at the Nationals. All year Steve wrestled at 190 and was champion at Richland and at U. of Wis. (Madison). Steve has lost only once all year in dual meets.

At 190 Randy Dockstader has given a fine showing for not having wrestled all year. He has qualified for nationals with a third place finish at Regionals.

Our H.V.T. Mike Kettman was champion at U. of Wisconsin (Madison) and took a second at Madison Tech. He has been very impressive and has gained birth at nationals having taken second at Regionals.

Hockey Season
Comes to an End

By BURTON B. COLLINS

"It's not whether you win or lose, it's how you play the game." According to Robert Cottingham, coach of the J.J.C. hockey team, our Wolves" came along way since October, they played good hockey throughout the year, and deserved a better fate;" the fate Coach Cottingham speaks of being a 1-15-1 won-lost record.

In the last two games of the season, against Ill. State, and Harper, the Wolves played .500 hockey. In the contest with Harper the Wolves trailed 4-0 midway through the second period, when they rallied with 2 goals by Dennis House and a single tally by Mike Kinder. However, they fell short of victory loosing 4-3.

Against Ill. State, the last game of the season, the Wolves led all the way after a first period goal by John Remegi, In the second period Dave Knutson scored two goals and Steve Allen added one as the Wolves held onto a 4-3 lead. Allen tallied again in the third period, his second goal of the year, and goalie Paul Jawarski turned in 20 minutes of shutout hockey, as the Wolves won 5-3.

According to Coach Cottingham "Next year looks very promising, as 12 out of this years 17 man squad will be returning."

Football Report
By JIM LOUKAS

On October 10 our Wolves ended their season on a sour note. The final score was 30-15. Coach Yost expressed that finally his team had played a bad game. There was no explanation but that the incentive was not totally there. Coach Yost stated that his squad looked second-class on the field. The old cliche, United we stand - divided we fall couldn't have been more true. The team not only was fighting Harper but also among themselves. Football is a very emotional sport and one never knows what will happen next.

Yost stated that excluding the game against Harper he could not have been any prouder. "This was the most cooperative and classiest team I have ever coached," so said Coach Yost. He also stressed that they are a great group of young men from the standpoint of individual personalities.

Even with the loss the Wolves still ranked No. 2 in the state with a 6-2 record and 17th or 18th nationally.

Football Honors Announced
Written by JIM LOUKAS

The final results for the 1973 football season can now be presented in its entirety. Football scores, all conference selections, all Region IV and an All-American nomination will be listed below. Congratulations men!

* Denotes Conference Game

```
* Morton 14 ....................................J.J.C. 28
* Illinois Valley ...............................J.J.C. 21
  Triton 12 .....................................J.J.C. 14
* Rock Valley 31 ...............................J.J.C. 21
* DuPage 17 ....................................J.J.C. 27
* Wright 6 ......................................J.J.C. 16
* Thornton 0 ...................................J.J.C. 28
  Harper 30 .....................................J.J.C. 15
```

6 wins   2 loses

Conference Record 5-1

Second Place in N4C conference

Rates second in state and 14 nationally.

All Conference Selections 1st Team Defense Tom Talarico L. B. Ken Dimke D. E.

1st Team Offense Doug Handorf H. B. Rusty Vincent F. B. Mike Kettman T. Craigh Phalen T. E.

2nd Team Offense John Popek C. Don Bejcek, Q.B.

All Region IV (State) Rusty Vincent, Doug Handorf, Ken Dimke, Tom Talarico

Honorable Mention All-Conference Jeff Olson

All American Nomination Ken Dimke

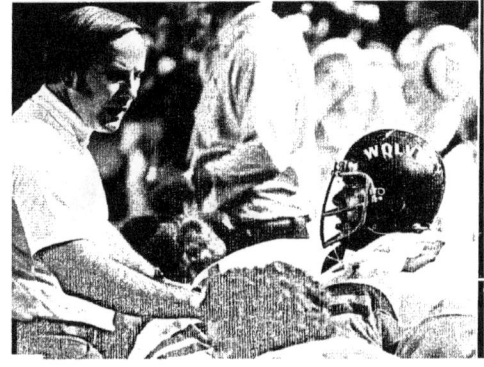

"moderate success" enjoyed by 73-74 basketball team

by paul riley
sports editor

"moderate success" that is how coach don tune summed up this year's basketball team.

establishing themselves with a 15 win 14 loss record tune gave what he thought to be the reasons for only this "moderate success".

1. eligibility problems: pete catchings and charlie jones were declared ineligible about half way through the season and thus we were without those 2 important men for about half of our games. tune said catchings was the big man we needed so desperately to be a top notch winner.

2. injuries: key personal were injured at critical times. bob herrod was lost for more than a month and missed some 7 games. tune said even at the end of the season herrod was not at full capacity. forrest harris also missed 4 games at critical times. both men sustained ankle injuries.

3. the schedule this year according to coach was probably as strong as joliet has ever played. he stated the n4c conference in his opinion is the strongest junior college conference as there is to be found in the entire state of illinois.

next year . . . well tune is hopeful with the return of gary rauch and bob herrod. these two have been recognized throughout the area as good, well rounded ball players.

cont'd on page

cont'd from page 88

end

across pages, left to right: frank lisdero, francis turner, karyl hamblett, kathy ferry

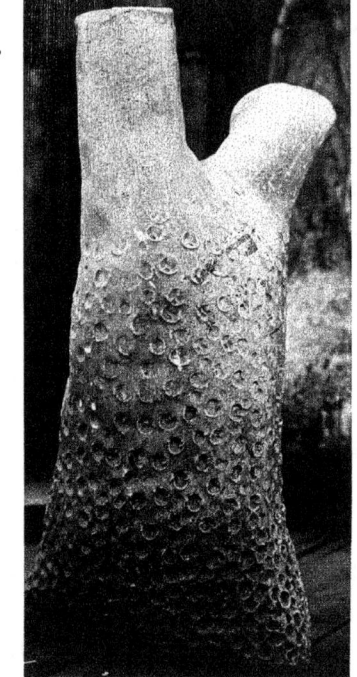

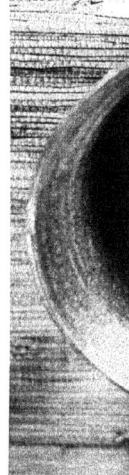

90

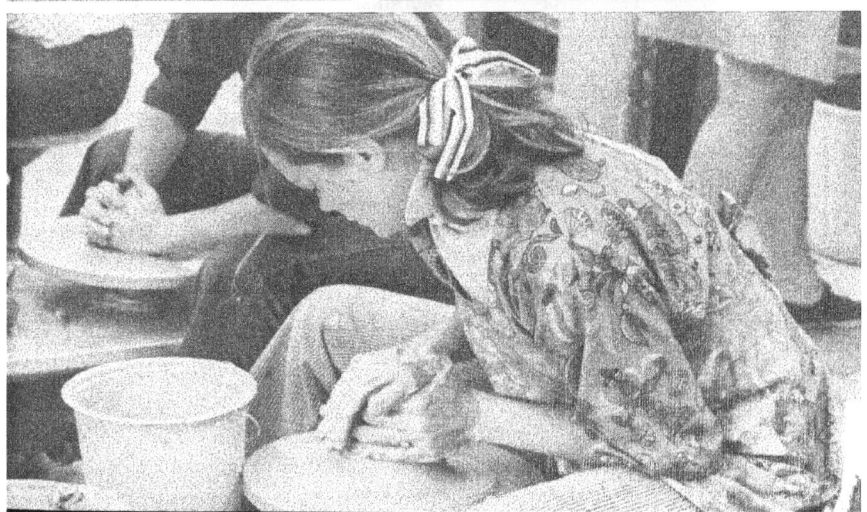

91

CAST IN ORDER OF APPEARANCE

Luanne Scholtes .... Catherine Reardon
Diane Forbes .... Mrs. Pentrano
Pete Graham .... Delivery Boy
Susi McCabe .... Cell Reardon
Sunny Grauer .... Anna Reardon
Louise Converse .... Fleur Stein
Dan Governale .... Bob Stein

TECHNICAL SUPPORT

Director .... Rosaline B. Stone
Technical Director ....Robert A. Mallary
Assistant to the Director .... Bill Greene

COSTUMES
  Mary Ann Governale

MAKE-UP
  Cindy Seng
  Mary Ann Governale
  Ellen McClure

LIGHTING
  Toni Tweedle
  Tom Reeves
  Linda Johnson
  Larry Kirin
  Rick Bush

SET
  John Parffrey
  All the JC Players

SOUND
  Larry Kirin

PROPS COMMITTEE
Sue Mitchell Chairman
Linda Johnson
Carol Sandretto

BOX-OFFICE
  Pam Bingaman
  Linda Dial
  Sue Hatzis
  Mark Selfridge
  Al Lentine
  Tom Reeves
  Dave Zordan
  Thom Smith

PUBLICITY & PLAYBILL
  Thom Smith
  Debbie Lacjin
  Connie Williams

HOSPITALITY
  Mickey Moore
  Al Lentine
  Paul Rittof

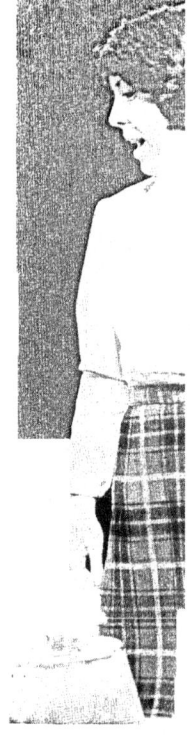

by

march 7
joliet juni

ABOUT THE PLAYERS

The assistant to the director is **BILL GREENE.** A freshman at JJC, Bill is studying theatre. He appeared in several high school plays at Lockport Central and also Tangerine Tent. Here at JJC Bill worked on **Butterflies Are Free**, and most recently was seen as Herr Schultz in **Cabaret.**

PETE GRAHAM plays the delivery boy. A freshman, majoring in engineering, he later plans to attend the U of I. Previous theatre experience includes plays a Joliet West, Curbside, and last semester here at JJC when he appeared as Ernst Ludwig in **Cabaret.**

Anna Reardon is portrayed by **SUNNY GRAUER**, a freshman nursing major who wants to become a L.P N. Sunny's theatre experience comes from Joliet West where she worked primarily on make-up, but did appear in some shows. Here at JJC she has worked on **Butterflies Are Free** and **Cabaret.**

As Bob Stein, **DAN GOVERNALE** is making his debut here at JJC. Dan majors in English and hopes to someday enter the theatre professionally. He draws on his experience at Joliet Central where he appeared in several plays.

Playing the role of Mrs. Pentrano is **DIANE FORBES**, a freshman in liberal Arts. Diane's experience includes plays at Joliet Central and several contest plays. Diane most recently appeared as Fraulein Kost in **Cabaret.**

As Ceil Reardon, **SUSI McCABE** returns to the stage here at JJC. A freshman speech major, Sue hopes to obtain her degree in theatre and teach. Susi has appeared in plays at Joliet West, in California, and here at JJC.

LUANNE SCHOLTES is Catherine Reardon. Luanne is a liberal arts major with possible career plans in Art or English. Her experience in the theatre includes many plays here at JJC, including most recently **Cabaret.**

LOUISE CONVERSE plays Fleur Stein. A freshman English major, Louise plans to become a writer. Past experience in theatre includes plays at Joliet Central, and here at JJC. Louise was most recently seen in **Cabaret.**

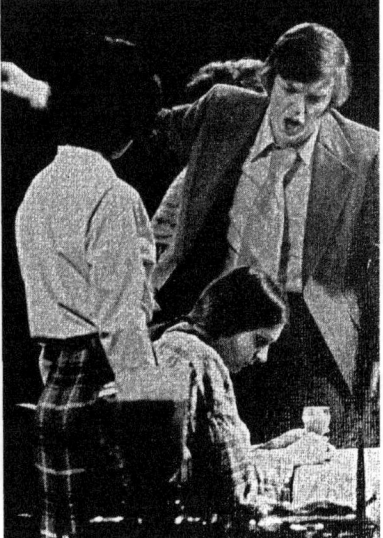

- dick jovonavich

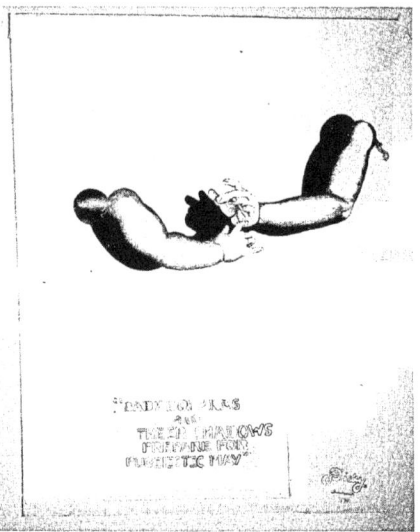

the 1974 shield staff extends its appreciation to the following people and departments without whose cooperation the '74 book could not have been realized: the art department; the music department; the english department; the wordeater staff and adviser, john stobart; the vocational technical department; athletic department; campus organizations and sponsors; mr. robert moorhead, walsworth publishing company; mr. joe cupp, walsworth publishing company; campus photo inc.; walsworth publishing company office personnel in marceline, missouri (shirley padgett, harold davolt); jjc's student affairs office and individuals whose work appears throughout volume I and volume II.

the staff; left to right: cindy getson, w.h. watling. dennis trowbridge, kathy cook, bob vroegindewey, liz higbee. adviser, bev shields

CPSIA information can be obtained
at www.ICGtesting.com
Printed in the USA
BVHW061336140119
537774BV00027B/1543/P